SIGN HERE IF YOU EXIST AND OTHER ESSAYS

Jill Sisson Quinn

MAD CREEK BOOKS, AN IMPRINT OF
THE OHIO STATE UNIVERSITY PRESS
COLUMBUS

Library of Congress Cataloging-in-Publication Data
Quinn, Jill Sisson, author.
Title: Sign here if you exist and other essays / Jill Sisson Quinn.
Description: Columbus : Mad Creek Books, an imprint of The Ohio State
    Univesity Press, [2020] | Summary: "Personal essays tying a woman's love of
    the natural world to her own experiences as an adoptive mother"—Provided
    by publisher.
Identifiers: LCCN 2020000083 | ISBN 9780814255926 (trade paperback) |
    ISBN 0814255922 (trade paperback) | ISBN 9780814278079 (ebook) | ISBN
    0814278078 (ebook)
Subjects: LCSH: Quinn, Jill Sisson. | Adoptive parents—Anecdotes. | Natural
    history—Wisconsin—Anecdotes.
Classification: LCC PS3617.U5644 A6 2020 | DDC 814/.6—dc23

LC record available at https://lccn.loc.gov/2020000083

Cover design by Angela Moody
Text design by Juliet Williams
Type set in Adobe Caslon Pro

♾ The paper used in this publication meets the minimum requirements of the
American National Standard for Information Sciences—Permanence of Paper for
Printed Library Materials. ANSI Z39.48-1992.

SIGN HERE IF YOU EXIST
AND OTHER ESSAYS

The Journal Non/Fiction Prize

for Tom and Beau

After a still winter night I awoke with the impression that some question had been put to me, which I had been endeavoring in vain to answer in my sleep, as what—how—when—where? But there was dawning Nature, in whom all creatures live, looking in at my broad windows with serene and satisfied face, and no question on her lips. I awoke to an answered question, to Nature and daylight.

—Henry David Thoreau, *Walden*

CONTENTS

ACKNOWLEDGMENTS

I gratefully acknowledge the publications in which portions of this book first occurred: *Ecotone* for "Sign Here if You Exist" and "The Myth of Home," *Orion Magazine* for "Metamorphic" and "Seeking Resemblance," *The Good Men Project* for "Think Like a Mountain," *New England Review* for "Big Night," and *Kenyon Review* for "Begetting."

SIGN HERE
IF YOU EXIST

The female giant ichneumon wasp flies, impressively for her near-eight-inch length, with the light buoyancy of cotton-wood fluff, seemingly without direction, simply aloft. Despite her remarkable size, she is not bulky. Her three-part body makes up only about three inches of her total length and is disproportionately slender; her thorax is connected to her abdomen by a Victorian-thin waist. Most of her maximum eight-inch span consists of an ovipositor half that length, which extends from the tip of her abdomen and trails behind her like a thread loose from a pant hem. Fully extended, she can be nearly as long as your *Peterson Field Guide to Insects*.

Her overall appearance of fragility—the corseted middle, the filamentous tail—portrays in flight a facade of drifting. But both of the times I have seen a giant ichneumon wasp, she was on a mission, in search of something highly specific: a single species among the nine hundred thousand described species of insects in the world (ninety-one thousand in the United States, eighteen thousand in Wisconsin, where I observed my second giant ichneumon). To comprehend this statistic, there are many things one needs to know: the definition of an insect, Linnaean taxonomy, the function of zero, the imaginary borders of states and countries. The female ichneumon wasp knows none of this. Yet it can locate a larva of the pigeon horntail—a type of wood wasp whose living body will nourish her developing young—hidden two inches deep in the wood of a dead tree, in the middle of a forest.

Charles Darwin himself, it turns out, studied the ichneumon wasp. He mentions it specifically in an 1860 letter to biologist Asa Gray, a proponent of the idea that nature reveals God's benevolence. Darwin, on the other hand, swayed no doubt by the rather macabre details of this parasitic insect's life, writes, "I cannot persuade myself that a beneficent and omnipotent God would have designedly created the ichneumonidae with the express intention of their feeding within the living bodies of Caterpillars"—and then, as if to reach the layman, he adds, "Or that a cat should play with mice." The tabby that curls in your lap and licks your temple, after all, has likely batted a live mouse between its paws until its brain swelled and burst. And the larvae of the giant ichneumon wasp eat, from the inside out and over the course of an entire season, the living bodies of the larvae of a fellow insect.

Like Darwin, I think I have put to rest my belief in a beneficent and omnipotent God, in any God really. Contrary to what I once believed, it is easy to let go of God, whose essence has never been more than ethereal anyway, expanding like an escaping gas into the corners of whatever church you happened to attend, into the breath of whatever frightened, gracious, or insomnious prayer you found yourself emitting. But it is much more difficult to truly put to rest the belief in an afterlife, the kind where you might get to visit with all your dead friends and relatives. It will not be easy to let go of your deceased mother, who stands in her kitchen slicing potatoes and roast, who hacks ice from the sidewalk with shovels; she is marrow and bone, a kernel of morals, values, and lessons compacted like some astronomical amount of matter into tablespoons, one with sugar for your cereal, another, for your fever, with a crushed aspirin and orange juice. You love her. You mark time and space by her: she is someone you are always either near to or very far from.

Can people live without the comfort of a creator? I think so. But relinquishing God—the Christian God, at least—does not leave everything else intact. A lack of the divine probably means that when you die, what you consider your essence will cease to exist. You will no longer be able to commune with the people you love. Choosing to live without the assurance of an afterlife, therefore, feels like a kind of suicide, or murder.

Most parasites do not kill their hosts. You—your living, breathing self—are evidence of this, as you host an array of parasitic microbes. Only about half of the 37.2 trillion cells in your body are really your own; the rest are bacteria, fungi, and other "bugs." The majority of these microbes are mutualistic, meaning both you and the microbe benefit from your relationship. Around five hundred distinct species of bacteria live inside your intestines. You provide them a suitable environment—the right moisture, temperature, and pH—and feed them the carbohydrates you take in. They shoot you a solid supply of vitamins K and B12, and other nutrients. But some microbes, like the fungi *Trichophyton* and *Epidermophyton*, which might take up residence beneath your toenails as you shower at the gym, are parasitic—they benefit from you, but you are harmed in some way by them. In the case of these two fungi, you would experience itching, burning, and dry skin. But you've probably never heard of anyone dying from athlete's foot, because it has never happened. Successful parasites—parasites that want to stay alive and reproduce—in general do not kill their hosts.

The giant ichneumon wasp is one of few parasites that break this rule. Actually, it is not a parasite at all; it is more correctly called a parasitoid because its parasitism results in the death of the host. This is not to say the ichneumon wasp is not successful. It can afford to kill its host because its host has a rapid reproduction rate. If we did not have the ichneumon wasp, we also might not be living in wooden houses, because the wood-boring insects these wasps parasitize would probably have killed all the trees. The wasp might look formidable, but in terms of its ecological role, it is a friend to humans.

This is what it does: a new giant ichneumon wasp hatches from its egg in a dark, paneled crib deep inside a dead or dying tree where the pregnant female placed it. Nearby, or sometimes directly beneath the egg just deposited, lies an unsuspecting horntail larva that has been chewing its cylindrical channels in the wood for sometimes two years. The wasp baby latches on to the exterior of the caterpillar and feeds on its fat and unvital organs until both are ready to metamorphose into adults. Then, when the host has chewed the pair nearly to the surface of the tree and the giant ichneumon wasp larva, which cannot chew wood, has a clear exit, the ichneumon kills and consumes its host. The wasp metamorphoses, possibly over the course of an entire winter, then emerges. Often before the newly metamorphosed females have even passed through their exit holes, they will mate with one of the plethora of males that have alighted on the bark for just this purpose. It's a kind of ichneumon *quinceañera*, a spontaneous debutante ball.

✳

The problem of where I would go after I died began with simple arithmetic. In our family there were five—my mother, my father, my two older sisters, and me. Yet the world never seemed to divide by fives or threes as easily as it did by twos: I stood *between* the double sinks my sisters occupied when we brushed our teeth; the chair where I sat for breakfast, lunch, and dinner was pulled up to our oval table just for meals, positioned at a point not opposite anyone, and then pushed away when we were done—it didn't even match our first dining room set; I sat in the middle of the backseat of the car, while my sisters each got a window; and when we bought a dozen donuts, the last two always had to be divided, somehow, into five equal pieces—or three, which was no easier, if my parents were dieting. At some point in my childhood, for some unknown reason—I have asked them, and they still can't say why—my parents bought four burial plots. I couldn't make any sense of this. I worried. Where would the last one of us who died—probably me—be laid to rest? All I could foresee was my parents and sisters lined up neatly next to one another for eternity. All I could do was fear my impending, everlasting physical absence from the people I loved most. Now that my sisters and I have married and they have had children and I have moved away, I realize the accounting error was not in buying too few but in buying too many: there will likely be two empty plots next to my parents. I've become accustomed to physical distance from my nuclear family by settling eight hundred miles from where I grew up, but the problem of where I will go after I die, what I will be like, and who will be with me has not gone away. It has only magnified.

Megarhyssa, the Latin name for the genus to which the giant ichneumon wasp belongs, translates to "large-tailed."

The species that I saw was likely *Megarhyssa macrurus,* which translates to "large-tailed, long-tailed." These genus and species names, then, provide no information that an observer couldn't pick up in a single, fleeting interaction with the insect itself. The tail is more precisely called an ovipositor, an appendage used by many female insects—and some fish and other creatures—to place their eggs in a required location. That place might be soil, leaf, wood, or the body (inside or out) of another species.

The ichneumon's process of depositing eggs with her long ovipositor goes from mystical to complicated to bizarre. First, she locates her host by sensing vibrations made from its chewing beneath the wood. Her antennae stretch out before her, often likened to dowsing rods, occasionally tapping the bark, and she divines the presence of the horntail, catches it snacking like a child beneath the bedsheets after making a midnight trip to the kitchen. She "listens" for the subsurface mastication of an individual caterpillar encapsulated in old wood.

Now the pregnant female begins the increasingly complex actions that will transport the eggs from her body through as much as two inches of woody tissue to the horntail's empty channel. Keeping her head and thorax parallel to the wood, which she grips with her legs, she first curves her abdomen under, into a circle, touching its tip to her thin waist. Her ovipositor, as if its outrageous length were not surreal enough, now performs a magician's feat: it separates into three long threads. The center one is the true ovipositor; the other two are protective sheaths that will help steady the insect's abdomen and guide the ovipositor as it enters the wood. (When she is finished laying and flies off, you will sometimes see these three threads trailing separately behind her.) The two sheaths, one on each side, fold back and follow the curve of her abdomen, then come together again at the tip of her thorax and head straight for the wood, sandwiching her body in two broadly looped capital Ps. The ovipositor extends directly into the two sheaths where they join and disappears between them. In order to allow the ovipositor's acrobatics, the exoskeleton at the tip of the abdomen splits somewhat and pulls back. At this stage in her laying, with her ovipositors perpendicular to the tree, her wings flat and still, and her legs spread-eagle, the ichneumon looks as if she has pinned herself to the wood as an entomologist might pin her to a cork for observation.

Before we hang up from our once-weekly phone call, my mother says she has one more little story to tell. This one is about Kristen, my niece, at age five my mother's youngest granddaughter.

The week before Easter, she and Kristen drove to the church where my grandparents and my mother's little brother, who died when he was a baby, are buried. My mother wanted to put flowers on the headstones. Before they got out of the car, Kristen began talking about her own mother and her older sister, Katie.

"Mommy and Katie want the same," Kristen said, "but I want to be different."

"What do you mean?" my mother asked.

"I want to be buried," Kristen replied. "But Mommy and Katie want their bones—" She paused for a minute, thinking, then continued. "They want their bones burned." Kristen paused again, then concluded, "But, really, I don't want to die."

My mother said she had to stifle a laugh. And I laughed, too, when she related Kristen's words. Yet I can't help but think our laughter was cover for some deeply rooted disquiet.

It's merely the brain's best method for dealing with this cruel yet basic fact of life—that it ends—stated here so rationally by a little person just in the process of recognizing it.

My mother, always prepared for the teachable moment, put forward to Kristen, "Well, Jesus is going to give you your body back, you know."

Kristen was not appeased. "That's weird," she replied.

The intricacy—and weirdness—of the ichneumon's egg laying makes it difficult for most of us not to wonder who came up with the complex series of steps involved. Part of that is because humans seem to be, as professor of psychology Paul Bloom puts it, "natural-born creationists." His essay "In Science We Trust," from the May 2009 issue of *Natural History*, posits that where humans see order—anything that is not random—we immediately assume an intelligent being has created that order. Bloom sums up the research beautifully: children aged three to six who were shown pictures of both neat and messy piles of toys, along with a picture of a teenage girl and a picture of an open window with curtains blowing, reported that both the sister *and* the wind could have caused the messy pile, but only the sister could have stacked the toys neatly; likewise, shown a cartoon of a neat pile of toys created by a rolling ball, babies as young as one year old stared longer than normal, which, according to developmental psychologists, indicates surprise.

Once, at the mouth of a sizable hole along a favorite trail, I found a mashed garter snake, a flattened mole, and a deceased opossum. They were each uneaten and—I knew intuitively—could not possibly have all died there coincidentally. Rather, I soon found out, they were a stack of "toys," planted neatly by a mother and father fox at the den entrance, to occupy their kits in the dusk and dawn while the parents hunted and scavenged for food. (When the family moves to a new den, which they frequently do, the parents move the toys as well.) A pile of sticks pointed on both ends, with the bark removed to reveal the white wood underneath, mortared together with mud and lined up across a stream has never been the work of the wind in the entire history of the earth but always the work of an intelligent being—*Castor canadensis,* the American beaver.

But being "created" does not inherently imply the existence of a creator, as evidenced in Darwin's work on natural selection. Bloom explains, "Darwin showed how a nonintelligent process driven by random variation and differential selection can create complex structure—design without a designer." So this instinctive assumption that complexity is the work of an intelligent being is true *most,* but not *all,* of the time.

Natural selection, though, in itself, does not inherently negate the existence of a creator. It is possible to imagine that a creator put into motion several set laws—the laws of Newton, for instance, and the laws of natural selection—then, without interfering, let creation unspool itself.

But even this belief begs a question. I asked my mother this question once, when I was seven or eight. We were in the car, on the way home from my organ lesson. "What was there before God?" I asked. "Who created him?"

"There was nothing," my mother said, and her hands left the steering wheel for a moment. Her fingers spread like the fingers of an illusionist, as if she were scattering something, everything in the known world, I guess. These religious discussions of ours were delicate and infrequent, almost, like discussions of sex in our family, too intimate to occur between parent and child. When we did have them, it felt as if we were uncomfortably close to uncovering something—for her, something too hallowed to be near; for me, something possibly too tragic. "I know," she conceded, "it's hard to imagine."

But I did imagine it, using the only sequencing skill I had then: a two-frame comic strip. In the right frame there was a profile of a cartoon God, and in the left frame, just blackness.

Megarhyssa macrurus is a mixture of mustard yellow and auburn, with chestnut brown accents. From a distance, the wasp may look just dark, but pinned as the female is during egg laying, and patient as the male is when waiting for the virgins to emerge, you can easily get close enough to notice the mostly yellow legs, yellow- and auburn-striped abdomen, and brown antennae and wing veins.

When the female is well into her egg laying and possibly at the point of no return, she becomes even more colorful and, at the same time, more bizarre. We left her with her three tails separate and in position, and her abdomen curled in a downward circle. Once it is time to deposit the eggs, she uncurls and raises her abdomen so that it is nearly perpendicular to the tree and her body. Her tails remain in their same positions. But two of the segments near the tip of her abdomen open wide, like the first cut in an impromptu self-cesarean section, revealing a thin yellow membrane. The membrane, taut like the surface of a balloon, is about two centimeters in diameter. It pumps gently. It is as attention-getting as a peacock's display but wetter, more intimate. Within that membrane you can see what look like portions of the ichneumon's three tails as they exist *inside* her body. Though the ovipositor appears to begin at the tip of her abdomen, as an appendage—like an arm or a leg or a tail—it must in fact be more tongue-like and extend into her inner recesses. It's as if you're witnessing an X-ray, but even so, it's difficult to figure out exactly what is going on. There are too many parts, too many steps, too much intertwining. Watching the ichneumon lay her eggs is like trying to decipher one of those visual-spatial problems on an IQ test: if the following object is rotated once to the left and twice vertically, will it look like option A, B, or C? Give me the 3.5 billion years that natural selection has had—whether here or in the afterlife—and I just might figure it out.

✳

Belief in an afterlife, and the manner of behavior, prayers, rituals, and burial practices necessary for navigating one's way to it, can be considered universal in human cultures. But belief in an afterlife cannot be considered the essence of all religions. Certainly there were cultures obsessed with it—the Egyptians, for instance, who took part in elaborate processes of mummification in order to preserve the dead and aid them in making the physical journey to heaven. But, hard as it may be for Christians, for whom a belief in resurrection and the afterlife takes center stage, to understand, other cultures and religions either simply didn't address the afterlife or had a less-than-attractive view of it. Those who originally penned the Hebrew Bible, for example, did not conceive of any type of survival after death; God harshly punished those who did not listen to his Word in this life with plagues, fevers, famine, and exile, and rewarded those who did with immortality only through their physical descendants. Were natural selection an option for the early Hebrews, I believe they would have been more accepting of the theory than today's Americans.

Other cultures did conceive of an afterlife, but not the type that came as a reward for moral behavior or religious faith or acceptance of a certain savior. For the Babylonians and the ancient Greeks, immortality was reserved for the gods alone. Death for mortals meant a sort of eternal, shade-like, underground existence, where food and water would be merely sufficient. Incidentally, the Babylonian "afterlife" was so unappealing that it actually became the paradigm for hell in Christianity.

The concept that an afterlife is a reward for, or at least related to, moral acts carried out in this life was made popular by Plato and later by Judaism, Hinduism, Buddhism, Christianity, and Islam. In Hinduism and Buddhism, one can achieve immortality only by breaking the cycle of rebirth, something I am not sure, were I Hindu or Buddhist, I would even want to do. (The only thing more comforting to me than a religion with an afterlife would be the ability to exist on Earth forever; returning even as a dung beetle could be quite exhilarating for someone who'd already had thrills at observing eight-inch wasps in this life.)

An appendix to *How Different Religions View Death and Afterlife,* by Christopher Jay Johnson and Marsha G. McGee, contains my entire former worldview. In response to the question of if we will know friends and relatives after death, the spokesman surveyed on behalf of the United Methodist Church says, "We will know friends and relatives in the afterlife and may know and love them more perfectly than on Earth." This was a worldview I picked up during sixteen years of thirty-minute, weekly lessons in a tiny basement Sunday school room at Patapsco United Methodist Church, where my mother was organist and my parents purchased their bewildering number of burial plots. The church was high on a hill above a creek and across from a junkyard, whose collage of rusted colors I viewed every week through the window during Sunday services: old cars tethered to the earth by kudzu and honeysuckle, seemingly inert but easily unfettered when a father or brother came in search of a hubcap, a passenger's door. Belief in an afterlife has been the grounding expectation of my existence, the hope I find so hard to give up even after giving up the Father, the Son, and the Holy Ghost.

✳

Before and even throughout my adolescence, I was a believer. I'd always held a sort of patient expectation for the Second Coming or some other miracle. As soon as I learned to write, I tried to speed things up a bit. *Sign here if you exist,* I wrote to God on lined white paper in a collage of yellow capital and lowercase letters. The color, which made the note barely legible, was not chosen for its symbolic connotation—enlightenment—but never even considered, in the way that children, caught up in the greatness of an act, overlook the details necessary to achieve it. I slid the note under my dresser and checked it every day. One morning, I found that God had answered.

There came a moment of astonishment, then almost assurance, when I pulled the note from its hiding place. But too soon I recognized the blue Bic pen, the neat, curvy letters, the same arcs from the thank-you notes Santa wrote for the cookies we'd left him. Perhaps I would have believed it was God who'd answered if my mother would simply have done what the letter requested. Instead she wrote me a note about love and faith, probably a series of *x*'s and *o*'s, like she put in our valentines. She was, and is, a believer; she would not forge his name.

✳

Tim Lewens, author of *Darwin,* a book that deals with the impact Darwin's thinking has had on philosophy during the last 150 years, has discussed the same question I asked my mother in the car as a child on the way home from my organ lesson. Although the question applies to any type of creator, in Lewens's interview for the Darwin Correspondence Project, he specifically addresses the idea of the laissez-faire God who sets up the laws of physics and natural selection and then lets them do their own work, the kind of God who might appeal to most scientists, the God that Darwin himself, Lewens says, likely believed in.

To deal with this question, Lewens draws from the rationale of philosopher David Hume. If you subscribe to this type of God, you are still left with the question of who or what was responsible for God, and who or what was responsible for whoever or whatever was responsible for God, and so on down the line, endlessly. At some point, Lewens says, if you want to be a theist, you have to stop asking the question of what came before God or created him and just accept his existence as—in Lewens's own words—a sort of "brute, inexplicable fact." And if you allow for the existence of brute, inexplicable facts, then you might as well just accept the brute, inexplicable laws of physics and natural selection. If the only purpose for a creator is to set into motion the laws of science, Lewens asks, then why on earth do you need one? According to Hume and Lewens, whether God exists or not doesn't solve anything.

When the question of a creator's existence became for me just a matter of semantics and personification, it was easy enough to put the idea of that creator to rest. Would the ichneumon become any less immanent if it were created not by some*one* called God but by some*thing* called natural selection? Both require faith of a sort. This part of the equation is easy, but I find it much harder to let go of the one thing God gave me that I coveted: an afterlife, and a clear path to it. I blame nature for this.

About a week after my second sighting of an ichneumon, I encounter another on the same path, on the same tree, in what I have come to call the "pinned" position. I wait for her to curve her abdomen up, split it open, and reveal its inner workings, but I see no movement. I poke at her gently with a twig. She barely stirs. (I have read that occasionally during the drilling process, which can take half an hour, a wasp's ovipositor will become stuck in the wood, and she will be left there, a snack for some predator that will pluck her body from her tail as if detaching a bean from its thin tendril. The ovipositor is left protruding from the wood like a porcupine quill.) A week later she is gone, and yet another ichneumon is performing her ancient task, already flexing the yellow circle. She is close to the ground, and the leaf of a small plant is obstructing my view. When I attempt to move it, my thumb and forefinger coming at the wasp like a set of pincers, she bats at me with her front legs, then takes off, detaching herself fully from the wood. Her membrane looks like a tiny kite. Her ovipositor and its sheaths, as well as her body, still warped into laying position, are like distorted and cumbersome tails, yet she flies, unimpeded, up and up, as if to another world.

※

Once, when I was nine or ten, I opened the screen door to share with my dog, who was lying on the back porch, the remnants of a grilled-cheese sandwich that I couldn't finish. The family parakeet, Sweetie, was perched on my head. The scene must have looked Garden of Eden-esque: a primate accompanied by a parrot feeding a canine. But I'd forgotten about the bird in my hair, and when I opened the door he escaped to a high branch on one of the oaks that grew behind the clothesline. A crow landed next to him, looking huge and superhero-ish. Nothing could coax Sweetie to return, not even his open cage, which for the next several days we stood next to in the yard, calling his name. Immediately after his escape, I had run into the forest in tears and was gone for the afternoon. Later, on the porch steps, I asked my mother if Sweetie would go to heaven.

Like many years before, she could not lie.

"The Bible tells us that animals don't have souls," she replied. Perhaps seeing my devastation, she added, "But it also says that God knows when even the smallest sparrow falls."

✳

According to Alan F. Segal in *Life After Death,* my position is not unique: more Americans believe in an afterlife than in God himself. Furthermore, the General Social Survey he cites, conducted by the National Opinion Research Center, shows that Jewish belief in an afterlife has jumped from 17 percent (as recorded by those born between 1900 and 1910) to 74 percent (as recorded by those born after 1970). Segal's hypothesis, which is that a culture's conception of the afterlife reveals what that culture most values as a society, fits right in with these statistics. Americans define themselves as defenders of freedom and individual rights. We believe we should be happy, wealthy, and healthy all the time. Why, then, even after giving up God himself, or even when subscribing to a religion that doesn't pay much attention to the afterlife, would we consent to imprison ourselves with mortality? Why would we give up our individual right to eternal life?

Paul Bloom would attribute my tendency to believe in life after death simply to being human. Humans, Bloom maintains, seem to be born already believing in an afterlife. In his essay "Is God an Accident?" published in *The Atlantic* in December 2005, he argues that humans are natural dualists. He does not mean that we are born with a Zoroastrian belief in the opposing forces of good and evil, but that we hold two operating systems in our minds—one with expectations for physical objects (things fall down, not up) and another with expectations for psychological and/or social beings (people make friends with people who help them, not people who hurt them). These expectations are not learned, but built-in, and can be observed in babies as young as six months old. These two distinct, implicit systems cause us to conceptualize two possible states of being in the universe: soulless bodies and, no less possible, just the opposite—bodiless souls. The two systems are separate. Therefore, when a human's body dies, humans are predisposed to believe that the soul does not necessarily die with it. Bloom cites a supporting study by psychologists Jesse Bering and David Bjorklund, in which children who were told a story about a mouse that was eaten by an alligator rightfully believed that the mouse's ears no longer worked after death and that the mouse would never need to use the bathroom again. But more than half of them believed the mouse would still feel hungry, think thoughts, and desire things. Children, more so even than adults, seem to perceive psychological properties as existing in a realm outside the body, and therefore believe these properties exempt from death. According to Bloom, "The notion that life after death is possible is not learned at all. It is a by-product of how we naturally think about the world."

I want my mother to read Bloom's essay. I'm not sure why. Throughout her childhood my mother walked of her own volition up the hill from her house to go to the little church across from the junkyard. Her mother and sister went; her father and much younger brother did not. When she was nine or ten she was chosen by Mrs. Myrtle, the church organist, to receive free piano lessons. My mother had an old upright piano in her family's unheated front room. Some of the keys did not play, so the ramshackle instrument was eventually chopped up for firewood. Then she had to practice at Mrs. Myrtle's, and was sometimes politely sent home when she played too long. My mother has been the volunteer organist at Patapsco United Methodist for more than thirty years.

She is sixty-two years old. Why, at this late stage, do I want to push Bloom's essay into the face of her contentment? Why does it feel slightly cruel, as though I am a bully, and why do I want to do it anyway?

I bring "Is God an Accident?" with me during a summer visit. The first page has been somehow lost on the plane, and I have to make a special trip to the local library to download and print out another copy. I'm hesitant to give my mother the essay, but when I find her one afternoon on the couch preparing for her Bible study—they've reread the entire book of Genesis, she says—it feels like an open invitation. She puts the essay to the side to read later, and the discussion that ensues between us is as unfulfilling, as inconclusive, as this discussion is everywhere—in high school biology classrooms; in rural, local papers' letters to the editor. It ends only with her decreeing, exasperated, "Your faith is stronger than mine." She does not mean my faith in natural selection, but my faith in God. She believes, perhaps counterintuitively, that all of my research and questions indicate some sort of allegiance to the religion I was raised with, or, at the very least, an inability to simply cast it aside.

My mother could live for forty more years, another entire life, longer than my own life has been so far. Or she could be dead in just eight years, at seventy, before her youngest grandchild reaches high school, possibly before she meets any child of mine. The current life expectancy for American women lies somewhere in the middle of that. Of course, I know I could die in the next fifteen minutes from a brain aneurysm, or be murdered by the man tuning my piano, but those are exceptions, and each would be a shock. If I were certain of the afterlife, what should not be a shock, what should be normal, is this: *our mothers are going to die, and for a while we are going to have to live without them.* But if I abandon my belief in life after death, am I putting my mother to rest before I really have to?

My mother tells me about an email she sent to another of my nieces, Julie, who is seventeen. Julie had just lost her guinea pig, Charlie, a faithful pet for seven years. Twice in the last month she had found him lying in his cage with his neck askew, unable to move. The second time, he died the next morning.

My mother wrote to Julie that she would never forget her cutting up vegetables for Charlie and making his daily salad. *He had a good life,* she wrote, *and you just might see him again one day.*

I can't help but notice the difference between my mother's unsolicited response to Charlie's death and her answer to my direct question years ago, of whether my escaped and presumed-dead parakeet would eventually make it to heaven. Perhaps, with age, my mother's views have softened a bit. Honesty has become less important than comfort. What she would like to believe has superseded what she once took as fact. We come to see that death is less about losing the self than about losing what was built between selves when they were alive. When she dies, my mother will be in a casket on the hill outside Patapsco United Methodist. The question I would like to ask is *will we find each other again*? But that is not it at all. Rather, I must find a way to live now knowing that one day we will no longer be mother and daughter.

✳

Now that I have discovered the ichneumon nursery standing in my woods, I will revisit it often. In spring I want to see the newly metamorphosed wasps born from the horntails' tunnels, these burrows that double as grave and womb. I'd like to see how many will emerge, how big they are, how long they rest on the dying tree before their first, seraphic flight. I'd like to search for whether there is any evidence of the horntail larva that nourished them—an exoskeleton, perhaps—or whether the larva is now present somehow only in the new body it has helped to form. All winter I will anticipate the decaying oak's promise: the giant ichneumon wasps' emergence.

There is life, it seems, after death—but it may be only here on Earth. Nature provides too many metaphors for us to so easily give up on this idea. It pummels us with them season after season and has done the same to others, I suppose, for thousands of years, playing on the human mind's ability to compare unlike things in its search for truth. I once shook a nuthatch from torpor on the side of a red pine, where it had stood unmoving, facedown—as only its kind can—all through my breakfast after a night of below-zero weather. I lifted a mourning dove, seemingly frozen into my cross-country ski trail during a surprise snow squall, in my own two palms, from which it flapped, as if from Noah's own hands. In my parents' woods, where my mother pitched a flower left from her mother's funeral, a patch of daffodils came up the next year—and has come up every year since—on its own, through a foot of dry leaf litter, shaded and unwatered. And there is the freezing and thawing of wood frogs in northern climes; the hibernation of chipmunks and groundhogs and jumping mice; the estivation of turtles in summer; metamorphoses of all kinds, but in particular the monarch butterfly (what Sunday school classroom has not used this metaphor at Easter?); the dormancy of winter trees; the phases of the moon; the seasons themselves; sleeping and waking; monthly bleeding; and, though it is too early to remember, probably birth, even.

This is what it comes down to. My mother, in giving me life after birth, also engendered in me the idea of God, and the unstoppable desire for life after death. We live on an earth where it seems nearly impossible for humans to have ever avoided inventing heaven, an earth that throws things back at us so reliably it is hard not to imagine that one day we will be resurrected, too, and that we will live forever. *Sign here if you exist,* I once wrote, but the question of whether God exists is really a question of whether *we* do. Without God and the promise of resurrection, you become extremely short-lived. Or the other option: you live forever, but what you currently perceive as yourself is a mere phase, a single facet: once oak, now horntail, soon-to-be ichneumon.

What type of afterlife do I need to survive—not so much in the next life, I realize now, but to get me through this one? I got my elements from stars: mass from water, muscles from beans, thoughts from fish and olives. When Edward Abbey died, his body was buried in nothing more than an old sleeping bag in the southern Arizona desert. He said, "If my decomposing carcass helps nourish the roots of a juniper tree or the wings of a vulture—that is immortality enough for me. And as much as anyone deserves." Abbey is right.

Your trillions of cells—only half of which, remember, were yours anyway—will become parts of trillions of things. And even that half wasn't really yours to begin with. You were only borrowed. We've had it backward all along: the body is immortal—it is the soul that dies.

THE MYTH OF HOME

This lake believes it is the ocean. It speaks the same language—a tongue like wind, the only word an unceasing sibilance. Ring-billed gulls search for arthropods and fish, wings bent earthward at the wrists like paper airplanes made by smart boys. Their calls split the air, which smells cleanly of decay, brackish without the salt. Low, whitecapped waves of varying lengths in multiple rows strike shore like strings of Morse code. It isn't only the water that is unreadable. The sky scours the land for some kind of text, but the beach is covered in a sheet of sun-bleached *Cladophora,* algae woven by waves into one giant page. All it gives is confirmation of the rules in a childhood game: *Paper covers rock,* it says.

This is Lake Michigan. A crowded cedar forest, bark the color of kiwi skin shredding in long strips, opens to white dolomite bluffs. The only garbage, deflated party balloons— their once-bold foil colors now weather-muted—dot the cliff bottom. *Happy Anniversary!* they say to some distant individual. A chair that seems to have made its own self—legs, seat, arms, and back composed of the same angular white stones as the bluff—secures the shore.

I descend the accidental steps from our campsite, here at Wisconsin's Rock Island State Park, following my husband. Like a single animal we track along the shore; I, the hind legs, place my boots in exactly the spot his foot has just risen from. Suddenly it seems as if the mud-brown strap of his sandal has jumped off and is slithering toward the water. "Snake!" I yell. For a moment, mid-step, he straddles the animal, which has spun around to face us. Then with a high arc he safely rejoins his feet and turns to observe. The snake is a northern water snake, not an unusual inhabitant for a lake but a stranger to the ocean. Yet even the snake seems to be part of the ruse. His brown banding is barely visible, as if he is trying to camouflage himself within himself. He has curled into the infinity symbol. I want to believe what the snake says, that this water goes on forever, but I have learned to see the snake as a warning.

The first time I camped along a Great Lakes shoreline was in Michigan's Upper Peninsula. From sandstone cliffs I stared down two hundred feet at water the green of oxidized copper. Lake-bottom stones, their size diminished by distance, stared back at me through the deeply transparent water like coins in a shopping-mall fountain. Water spilled through narrow nooks in the cliff tops and fell in powerful, gradually widening streams directly into Lake Superior as in the introduction to the '80s TV show *Fantasy Island*. When I sent pictures and wrote about the trip to friends and family, I mistakenly called the place "Pictured Rocks National Seashore." *Where is this seashore?* my friends asked. *Oops— lakeshore,* I retyped. I couldn't help feeling like it was a downgrade. But more than that, I was surprised at the ease with which I, an east coaster, had made the error.

What would it be like to meet this lake on its own terms, having traveled no more than to and from its own shores— oceans, at best, a distant mythos? I wish to be indigenous to every place I visit, to see it as Earth entire. How nice it would be to shed the compulsion to compare one landscape to another, to analyze, evaluate. To simply hear what the land says. To no longer have to choose or love or hate, to let down my guard and feel the power of the sea in this Great Lake.

I was not born of the ocean. The sea was more great-aunt than mother. Her strange manners—the continuous roar of her voice, how she would grab hold and pull me wherever she was going—always left me a little afraid. But during my yearly visits, I would come to love her eccentric ways: her salty smell, how light she made me feel when I was carried.

As soon as we crossed the Chesapeake Bay on the three-hour drive to Ocean City, Maryland, from my family's central Maryland home, I felt the land change. From the car window it appeared dismally flat. Only good for a bike ride, I thought. But when we reached our destination, I couldn't deny the power of the coast: the seeming bedside of the living Earth. At first, I played with the toys she scattered there—a clean, ancient soil, the smooth pieces of her inhabitants' homes. I was not sure what to think of her beckoning. Then, as I grew, I swam out beyond the breakers, and in a sort of reverse birth dove through the swells, feeling the rise and fall of her chest above me.

*

Post-snake, my husband and I explore Lake Michigan's shoreline further. I am unable to shake our discovery, surprised—stupidly, I quickly decide—to have stumbled upon a northern water snake in a Great Lake. I see such snakes all the time in the smaller lakes sprinkled across Wisconsin.

But here, unable to see this lake's opposite shore, beneath the gulls and with waves crashing in my ears, a horseshoe crab seems more appropriate. *This is not saltwater,* I remind myself. *This is not ocean.* The salt in Earth's oceans comes from volcanoes and hydrothermal vents, both ancient and active. It also comes from rain, rivers, and streams dissolving the sodium chloride in Earth's rocks and carrying it to the sea, where the average stay of a water molecule is hundreds to thousands of years, long enough for plenty of salt to accumulate as the water molecules that carried it there evaporate. Oddly enough, Earth's saltiest bodies of water are in fact lakes: Don Juan Pond in Antarctica is twelve times saltier than the ocean; Lake Assal in Djibouti is ten times saltier; and Utah's Great Salt Lake can be up to 7.7 times saltier. These lakes, though, like the oceans but unlike most other lakes, have no outflow. In the Great Lakes, a water molecule and its salts do not stay put for long—only about two hundred years—before traveling from lake to lake and then through the St. Lawrence Seaway to the Atlantic.

Nonetheless, there is still something faintly brackish about this Great Lake's air, and later, at home, I search for the logic behind my confusion. I chalk it up to the *Cladophora,* a normally translucent green, filamentous algae native to both marine and freshwater environments, ripped here by waves from its underwater home, churned into a mash deposited on shore, and combined with the exoskeletons of tiny crustaceans and the excrement of gulls. The shape of all this, I conclude—the same algae and gull poop, sand fleas and crabs swapped with crayfish and freshwater shrimp—must enter my nose and attach to the exact receptors as those molecules of sea air did so many years ago, a sort of skeleton key of odor, unlocking (salt or no salt) my brain's door to the ocean.

I laugh at what I am doing. I am unable or unwilling to submit to this lake's elemental power without proof of why it reminds me of an ocean. Regardless of how I may feel, I want empirical evidence. There is a caution I cannot shake, a fear that perhaps I am being tricked, a notion that the lake's power may be an illusion. Like a woman jilted at too young an age who will, for a split second, see her first lover's face on every male she encounters for the rest of her life, I have lost an innocence, an impressionability, I cannot reclaim. I fear that I will never be able to objectively see or properly love this lake.

A polar bear's home range can span 20,000 square miles— for reference, that's an area almost twice the size of Maryland, the state where I was born. A hedgehog, on the other hand, may live out its entire life within just a 120-yard radius of its nest. My mother lives within an obtuse, scalene triangle made up of an extremely short base: the distance between home and church (1.2 miles) and two relatively long sides: the distances (8.2 and 7.7 miles, respectively) between each of these places and the city of Westminster, Maryland, where she shops for groceries and deposits and withdraws money from the bank. My mother has occupied this small triangle of existence virtually all of her life, buying land and building a home with my father less than two miles from the home in which she grew up. It is consistent with the home range of hominids in the middle Pleistocene era, 126,000 to 781,000 years ago. Evidence in China reveals that these early humans found all the stones they needed for toolmaking within about a five-kilometer radius.

Whenever my family had to travel farther, my father was always the chauffeur. But trips were few and far between, and brief when they did happen. Our yearly trips to the beach, for example, usually lasted no longer than three days. I remember how happy my mother always was to come home, opening up the windows of the hot house as if lifting the lid of a coffin. And although I learned to love the ocean, I always suffered from a similar sort of hodophobia, though not so much a fear of travel as a feeling that travel was unnatural, even wrong. That we shouldn't be doing it. That the right thing to do was always just to stay home.

❋

Depending on what source you look at, Earth has between five and twenty biomes that you might call home. At minimum, Earth contains aquatic, desert, forest, grassland, and tundra environments. When only terrestrial biomes are considered, most sources agree on the overriding categories of desert, grassland, temperate deciduous forest, rainforest, taiga, and tundra. I grew up in temperate deciduous forest, and I still live in temperate deciduous forest now, in Wisconsin. One of these forests is near the ocean. But where I have lived, what I consider home, and where I have traveled—as much as they may have influenced me—are not the only factors affecting my appreciation of the landscape. Some research shows that, at least very early in life, the place we love most is a place we may have never set foot in.

❋

Rather than exploring the real coast of the lake that believes it is the ocean, my husband and I walk the perimeter of an island within it, an act decidedly more intimate, a kiss versus an embrace. The US has more coastline along the Great Lakes than along the Atlantic Ocean: 4,530 miles versus 2,069 miles. This fact, which includes only the US coastline of the Great Lakes and does not include the Gulf Coast of the Atlantic, was once interestingly illustrated by the Center for Ocean Sciences Education Excellence on their website dedicated to Great Lakes literacy. There, they had created a curious-looking map of the US by plunking the Great Lakes into the Atlantic Ocean and lining them up along the East Coast, beginning at Maine and extending just beyond the tip of Florida. The lakes had not been placed haphazardly; an attempt was made to match the nuances of the Atlantic coastline with the nuances of the coastline of each lake. The result, on first glance, was a map that depicted the Great Lakes as islands—an archipelago, a series of now-separate land masses that would fit with the continent as snuggly as South America once did with Africa. When I first looked at this map, I felt a strange affinity for the mapmakers. Perhaps, they thought, if we put the Great Lakes *in* the ocean, people will see the similarities. I'm not the only one, it seems, obsessed with comparison.

We might as well be standing on the coast of the Atlantic here, for the dolomite shore on this small island, part of the Grand Traverse Islands—an archipelago (such a marine-sounding word to me), which extends from the Door Peninsula in Wisconsin to the Garden Peninsula in Michigan—has opened up to a small beach of fine, white sand. A tiny town composed of an extended family's towels and umbrellas has sprouted near the water's edge. They will not need to pull their towels back later; the lakes do experience tides, but the tides are negligible—a fraction of an inch.

There are waves, though, caused by the same force as waves on the ocean—wind over open water—and my husband wants to swim, to bodysurf as he has in Florida, in Maryland. It certainly looks as if he could. He wades in. I snap a photo. Within the frame of my camera, his back to the shore, the picture has the same healing tone as a picture of the ocean. Once again I am fooled. It does not look as if he has entered into something, an enclosed body of water. It looks instead as if he is leaving, as if he has just shed an entire continent of worry.

I think about the original inhabitants of Rock Island, those who could truly be considered native: the Ottawa, Petun, and Hurons who fled here from Michigan in 1650 to avoid massacre by the Iroquois nation; the Potawatomi, who had already migrated here from across the lake ten years earlier; and the Native Americans who intermittently camped on this island's southern shore from as early as 600 BCE. Did they, having never seen its bigger, brinier cousin, experience this lake as an ocean? I imagine a Native American girl standing on the shore, hair blowing, the vastness before her not the smaller of two on a cerebral scale weighing bodies of water, but an icon of opportunity, the starting point of all possible journeys. If she started walking along its coast, who knew where she would end up? Certainly not back at her beginning, her entire cosmos circumnavigable. Her view included only the scene before her, no mental textbook open to a map of the world with its hemmed-in lakes and trailing ocean. When I look out over this water, I can feel what she must have seen: that veritable edge of the earth. But I can't see it as such. I know very little, but it is still too much.

Because the lake is too cold for anything more than wading (the average temperature for June in Ocean City, Maryland, where I grew up swimming, is 65°F; it's 56 in Lake Michigan in the same month), my husband and I spend the first hot, sunny afternoon of our two nights on the island reading and napping beneath the cliff that leads to our campsite. The next morning, rain and thunder keep us in the tent until around eleven a.m., at which time we begin the 5.2-mile walk around the island's perimeter on a forest trail that hugs the bluffs above the shore. The day is gray and damp, so we don't pass anyone for quite a while but gradually begin a game of hiker's cat and mouse with an older couple as we both pause to look at the same landmarks: foundations from a fishing village created by the island's first European settlers, a water tower, a family cemetery.

Finally, the older man says, "Have you been here before?"

"No," we respond. "Have you?"

"This is my forty-second time," he replies.

"Wow," one of us says, but he doesn't elaborate, so we push on toward the next landmark on our map: Wisconsin and Lake Michigan's first lighthouse. The ranger has informed us that volunteer docents give free tours in exchange for a week's stay in the lighthouse itself. "There's no electricity, and they have to pump their own water," he said. "But they keep coming back."

We are greeted by two barefoot, middle-aged women. They are surprised to see us in the dismal weather and ask us to remove our shoes before they lead us on a brief tour through the two-story, restored 1850s lighthouse, which once doubled as a home. It has been filled with early 1900s-style furniture, all the way up to the tower that now holds a replica of the lighthouse's original nine-sided lantern.

Curious about the volunteer program, we ask where they sleep.

"In the beds in these rooms," one of the women answers, pointing to the furniture we thought were museum artifacts. She tells us they have been acting as docents for several summers. They are cousins from Madison, and one of their ancestors was employed as a keeper here. He used to live in this home. They were not born of it, so I fantasize that an appreciation for the lake could somehow have carried through in their genes. And I wonder what the lake means to the man who has been here forty-two times, though I don't know where he, or his ancestors, are from.

✳

Once, when my father was unable to take off work, my mother and I had to drive the seventy-five miles from our home in Finksburg, Maryland, to the University of Maryland, College Park, near Washington, DC, where I was soon to start college. We were nervous, for we did not understand the language of the interstates: on- and off- ramps, the dreaded cloverleaf, signs that showed not the names of streets but cities we would never see that lay hours away at the ends of major thoroughfares.

Everything about the cloverleaf is counterintuitive to an earthly traveler. For a left turn, you *pass* the road you want, exit *right*, drive *back toward where you came from*, and only then merge onto the road you wanted to turn left on. Okay, I get it. But when I am holding myself onto the planet by gripping the steering wheel of a car moving seventy-five miles an hour, and I exit an interstate at a cloverleaf interchange, I feel I am lost in the ether. Unlike the homing pigeon, which faithfully flies in completely arbitrary directions in order to locate the magnetic lines or ultralow frequency sounds that will guide it back to its point of origin, my inner geometry breaks down. I have driven in a circle to make what should have been a right-angle turn. In a matter of seconds, I have occupied the same point of latitude and longitude in two different planes—by going over or under the road I wished to turn left on. Take an exit by accident, which we did, and in a matter of minutes I could be in another country altogether; for all I know, that centrifugal force on the exit ramp that pushes me to the driver's side window, making my seatbelt earn its keep—the same force that frequently topples eighteen-wheelers that exceed the cloverleaf's twenty-five-mile-per-hour speed limit—could be propelling me through time as well as space. Fortunately, on this day, we were able to navigate back to the interstate, to the college, and home again.

The only reason my mother and I were driving to the University of Maryland in the first place was because my parents had convinced me not to go through with the interview that I had scheduled at a college even farther away, in New York City. We delayed this interview for weeks. One evening, my mother stood at the doorway of my bedroom and said in a gently persuasive voice, "We have to drive through a tunnel *under a river* to get to this place." She knew who she was talking to. Driving over the Chesapeake Bay every year on the way to Ocean City always made me a little uncomfortable. *Under a river?* I thought. I had no compass for that. We couldn't afford this college anyway. "Cancel the interview," I said. And it was a good thing; utterly homesick, I would last only a year and a half at College Park before transferring closer to home and moving back in with my parents.

But as leery of travel as we might have been—as we still are—and as weird as travel has become in the modern age, we traveled. There were those three-day trips to the ocean, and one two-week trip to Disney World. My mother traveled to Tennessee on her honeymoon, and she has been to New Jersey, New York, and Wisconsin, where I live now, to visit me. I have flown over the Atlantic Ocean. Even I, my mother's daughter, no longer exist only in the smallest possible convex polygon drawn around my daily activities. I live in a world that drives and flies at unimaginable speeds and in all kinds of ridiculous shapes, and I wonder sometimes if all this whizzing by, encircling, and arcing over has somehow short-circuited my ability to appreciate the landscape.

We leave the Pottawatomie lighthouse (its spelling anglicized by European settlers)—an ironic name, as I imagine the last thing the Potawatomi wanted to do was guide in more European ships. Our next stop is the Viking Boathouse and hall, built by Hjortur Thordarson, an Icelandic man who moved to Milwaukee at age five, became a World's Fair–winning inventor, created Chicago's successful Thordarson Electric Manufacturing Company, and bought the whole island.

Just as we get to the building, I notice the western sky has darkened to a strange blue. The ranger appears to tell us a severe storm is coming; we can hear his weather radio beeping in the background, the calm, stoic voice contrasting eerily with the information it delivers: "This storm is capable of producing damaging hail and gale-force winds." It lists a series of towns and the estimated times the storm will pass through each one. Advising us to take cover in the boathouse, the ranger leaves to evacuate the campground.

The boathouse seems as if it were designed for giants. At one end is a human-sized fireplace, a sort of walk-in hearth. At the other, roped off, is the furniture Thordarson commissioned from Icelandic artist Halldor Einarsson: long oak tables and oversized, straight-backed chairs, each one carved with indecipherable runes and a scene from a Nordic myth. A few cases of Native American artifacts found on the island are displayed near the door. On the first floor, where we wait out the storm, arched windows nearly as large as the boat entries below, their bottom halves French doors, line three sides of the building.

We stare through the windows, watching the storm. Rain is already falling. According to the Environmental Protection Agency, storms on the Great Lakes can be more dangerous and more difficult to navigate than storms on the ocean. Storm waves in the lake, apparently, are more erratic compared to the mild rolling and swelling of the open sea. On November 10, 1975, the Edmund Fitzgerald—a 729-foot long,

13,632-gross-ton bulk carrier—sunk in Lake Superior in a storm that caused 25-foot waves. The entire crew of 29 was lost (and later immortalized in the Gordon Lightfoot song). In Buffalo, New York, at eleven p.m. on October 18, 1844, a 22-foot wave in Lake Erie broke the city's 14-foot seawall, flooding the shore and killing 78 people. The History Channel once aired a reality TV series called *Great Lake Warriors,* to rival the Discovery Channel's *Deadliest Catch,* a show that followed the adventures of five Alaskan king-crabbing boats on the perilous Bering Sea. "In the heart of America, on a deadly inland sea that has claimed as many as 6,000 vessels and 30,000 lives, a way of life exists that few ever witness," reads the description for *Great Lake Warriors* on the History Channel's website.

"What's that?" my husband says, just as I notice that way out over the water, something is moving toward us. The rain is coming at us horizontally, gray sheets of water and mist. It is as if we are looking at the edge of the approaching storm. I half expect to feel it strike, leveling the building, shattering windows. I am uncomfortable. I remember the first thunderstorm I felt somewhere other than my parents' house, standing on the green-carpeted staircase at my cousins', their second-floor playroom no longer so enticing. I feel the same unease now. Storms, I think—like most things—are best had at home. A door blows open. My husband reaches out an arm and attempts to pull it closed. At first, he can't do it. A tree on the shore bends willingly; a stubborn bench blows over. I fear for a moment I will lose him, but then he manages to pull it shut. An adventurous boy goes out in the downpour and jams the door closed with a stick. I think about our tent. I am sure by now it is floating upside down in Lake Michigan, like a giant balloon, no happy inscription across its colorful surface.

❋

Once, descending in a plane over Lake Michigan for a landing at Milwaukee's General Mitchell Airport, I looked forward and backward through the window and could see land
in each direction. "I can see both shores of Lake Michigan!" I
exclaimed to my husband. "We must be in the very middle."
He shook his head. "No," he said. "The lake is too big. You
couldn't possibly see both shores at once. We're just flying
over a corner of it." But, in fact, nothing on Earth is too far
away to be seen, as long as it is large enough. We can see
the sun, after all, which is ninety-three million miles away,
and at night the Andromeda Galaxy, which is 2.25 million
light-years away. The problem is the earth's curvature. It hides
things from view that the naked eye would otherwise be able
to discern.

Since then, I have found this simple but useful formula:

Distance Seen in Miles = 1.23 × √Your Altitude in
Feet

So we would only need to have been flying at 2,500 feet—
dangerously low—to be able to see 61 miles in all directions,
enough for me to have seen both sides of 118-mile-wide Lake
Michigan.

I don't know what I am trying to prove here. That Lake
Michigan is diminutive in size when compared to the ocean?
That you can swallow a Great Lake in one gulp, like a too-
small serving of dessert? Because what I felt from the plane
as we circled over that blue water wasn't derision but rather
awe, and not without confusion—similar to what I feel when
I stand before Lake Michigan here at Rock Island.

On that flight, the pilot had offered free TV. My husband
watched one of the limited options—*Real Housewives of New*

Jersey—but in the small screen flush with the seatback in front of me, I was tuned to the channel that showed our elevation and approximate location. We were at nine thousand feet. I pressed my forehead against the window and looked down at the wing, the lake. I was immediately taken in. The plane began to turn so that my gaze was nearly perpendicular to the water. A little sick, I kept looking. The lake had become impressionistic, like we were flying not over water but over the enlarged petal of a lupine or vinca. The tip of the wing looked deceptively low. We continued to turn, and the water slipped into focus. I could see ripples, but the plane's direction and the opposing flow of the current had canceled out any sign of movement. Now it appeared as if we were circling down onto the back of some exotic reptile, a skink perhaps, not just blue-tongued but blue-skinned, its cracked scales the color of water through a descending plane's window.

The scene blurred again. I must become an insect in a soda can hurled across a field, my brain a few simple nerves, in order to process what I see when I travel by plane: a reality show I just can't believe. If I really thought I was nine thousand feet above the middle of Lake Michigan—a ridiculously impossible point in space for a human to ever be—my fear of heights would kick in, as it did when I rode to the top of the St. Louis Arch. I would be afraid of falling into the water, not admiring the blue beneath me like some symbiotic insect about to land on the back of a skink. A little turbulence, the kind where the plane drops and someone screams and little kids laugh and your fellow passengers' heads swing from left to right in unison as in some sickly choreographed dance, can knock an awareness of the facts of flight into me like terminal illness sometimes shocks one back into a belief in God. But a smooth flight—the kind I always desire—a smooth flight is like a drug. It takes you somewhere with seemingly no price.

*

I have a friend who flies all the time. She and her husband, both teachers, spend entire summers in distant lands: India, Ghana. But sometimes, she tells me, she finds herself at an internet cafe in Bolivia planning her next trip to Indonesia. *Why can't I just enjoy every moment where I am?* she wonders. Her problem may not be exactly the same as mine. Still, it makes me consider that if I simply stopped traveling, I might be better able to connect with the land. And since I don't really like traveling anyway—by car or by plane—it seems like a simple solution. But no matter what land I am indigenous to or where I have or have not traveled, there may be other factors at work in determining what landscapes I prefer. Research shows that I will always, in some small way, pine for a place where I have never even been.

John H. Falk and John D. Balling compiled the evidence in their 2009 article "Evolutionary Influence on Human Landscape Preference." In countries all over the world, they note, artificial gardens and parks all exhibit the same design: expanses of well-cut grass sprinkled with trees. This is regardless of the surrounding biome in which the park is built. Worldwide calendar art of natural landscapes shows a similar preference. Cross-cultural studies indicate that humans also prefer the same type of tree: those with small, bifurcated trunks and big, leafy canopies. (The Japanese could even be said to have developed the entire horticultural art of bonsai based on this preference.) Falk and Balling believe this worldwide preference for an open, grassy, tree-studded landscape is actually a preference for savanna: Africa's five million square miles of rolling, relatively short-grass prairie dotted with small clusters of acacia trees, where the human family tree was planted six or seven million years ago.

To test their theory that humans' experience of natural landscapes is at least in part based on evolutionary principles, in 1982, Falk and Balling showed photographs of five major biomes—savanna, deciduous forest, coniferous forest, rainforest, and desert—to subjects in America. They found that subjects preferred savanna at least as much as their native biome and showed no preference for any of the other biomes. To mark out any cultural bias that Americans might have toward savanna-like landscapes due to exposure to parklands in urban settings, Falk and Balling replicated their experiment using subjects from Nigeria, whose home biome was primarily tropical rainforest. They got the same results. But more surprisingly, in their original study, Falk and Balling found that up until age twelve, children preferred savanna *over* their home habitats. This suggests that after many years of experience and enculturation, one can learn to love another biome. But no place on Earth can surpass the power of the savanna, the biome in which our ancestors evolved, to grip the human heart. Deep in our psyche, like the remnants of some long-forgotten affair, may lay the negative of an image reflected over and over in our ancestors' eyes: savanna, the face of our first provider.

Everything is still staked down when we finally make the soggy hike back to our campsite after the storm. "You're in the Black Forest!" the ranger had joked the other day while checking us in, referring to the woods of densely packed white cedar trees that housed our campsite and fire-ring; the forest, a windbreak and refuge, has kept our gear safe. We cook a wet dinner on my camp stove and then nature, like the capricious but loving mothers of modern memoir, brings

out the sun and raises our spirits. We take another hike along
the shore to search for the rock engravings we have read were
left on the cliffs by Thordarson's workers. We find one on
a crag on the southern end of the island: a depiction of a
Native American, naked, standing up to row a long canoe.

After viewing the engraving, we cut across a sand spit to
watch the sunset. Two cormorants—or loons, we can't tell
which—sit low in the water. Dull pink cumulonimbus clouds
show on the horizon like a distant badlands.

Back at our campsite again, though we've avoided getting
wet for the entire day, we consider taking a late evening dip.
After much thought, we climb down the bluff at the edge
of the Black Forest to the open lake. We strip naked, wading into the now-dark water. But the water is still cold and
its rocky bottom more hazardous in the low light. I slip and
land on my knee, and before we know it, we're back on the
shore, back in our clothes, up the bluff, and safe in the forest.

Falk and Balling's hypothesis about the human preference
for savanna also fits in with other proposals about landscape
appreciation. One of these is prospect-refuge theory, the logical idea that humans prefer landscapes with open vistas—
where they can detect potential hazards—as well as places
to hide. In the savanna, the vistas would be those long views
over the short grass prairie, and the hiding places would be
the clumps of trees.

Critics point out that new discoveries in the fossil record
indicate that the earliest humans didn't live solely on the
savanna, as previously thought. But DNA evidence suggests
that modern humans evolved from a small founder population of possibly only one thousand closely related individuals

living in the African savanna as recently as seventy thousand years ago. So, irrespective of what biomes our brethren lived in before then, you and I descended from inhabitants of the savanna. I may have to recast my conception of the Native American girl standing on the shore at Rock Island. Regardless of our knowledge of and feelings about Lake Michigan, we may be more similar than different in our view of the world, both infatuated with a landscape neither of us has ever traveled to.

I am torn. I would like my mother to visit me here in Wisconsin. And she has. To each place I have moved she has faithfully come—once—to see where I am eating and laying my head. Because she's reluctant to fly, she drove—or rather, my father did—the eight hundred miles to visit me one year after I moved, which, at the time of this writing, was eight years ago. Although we talk as if it might happen, I do not think it is likely that she will come again. There always seems to be a reason why they can't make it, and honestly, I don't blame them. Although I fly to Maryland four times a year to visit the family that I miss so much, the night before a flight, inevitably, that old fear rises in me again, the land like a magnet, the people I love secondary to my desire to stay put, both feet on the ground, racking up the data I need to make me feel at home. It still feels wrong to travel, to cover the eight hundred miles to my family in that two-hour plane ride, as if the land beneath me—between us—didn't matter. As if the terrain weren't an obstacle, weren't even real, my plane window a TV screen. In a plane, we gloss over the landscape like aloof gods who don't even believe in the existence of their own creations.

＊

The next morning, we are awakened in our tent at seven a.m. by a voice that is cheerful but urgent, almost as eerie as the robotic voice of the woman on the weather radio, its message the same. "Good morning! Campsite B! Anyone awake?" the ranger says. "Another storm like last night's is headed this way with seventy-mile-per-hour winds. It will be here in approximately thirty minutes. The shelter building is open!"

We can't believe it. I suggest we grab our breakfast so we have something to do while we wait out the storm in the boathouse.

"What?" my husband says. "No—this is it." And I know what he means. We were planning to catch the ten-o'clock ferry off the island today, so we might as well pack up all our sodden possessions now and still hope to make it to the boathouse before the rain. I put in my contact lenses using one of those impossibly small and blurry camp mirrors, then we deflate camp mats and stuff sleeping bags into compression sacks and then into our backpacks. At first I am wild with haste, but as the tent and its poles disappear compactly into their relative sacks, I realize we can probably get everything put away and make the one-and-a-half-mile hike to the boathouse safely before the storm hits. As we pack up our things, still in disbelief that we are again beset with the possibility of severe weather, we conjecture that maybe there is something inherently attractive about this island to storms. A half hour later, safe in the shelter, we look for confirmation. "Does the island get hit with storms like this a lot?" we ask the ranger. "Never in my sixteen years here have I had to evacuate twice in the same twenty-four-hour period," he replies, debunking our theory.

As I look out over the lake, I can't help but feel it is trying to tell me something by battering me with twin storms on this two-night camping trip. *Love it or leave it*, it seems to be saying. And why can't I? The National Oceanic and Atmospheric Administration tracks the same data for the Great Lakes as it does for the world's oceans. Detroit Public Television's two-hour film about the Great Lakes is titled *Freshwater Seas*. Some US citizens even refer to the Great Lakes as the "North Coast" or "Third Coast."

Are we doomed, in a sense, to always be comparers, always, like the cousins in the lighthouse and Chester Thordarson with his Icelandic Great Hall, refusing to forget that original habitat, the land of our ancestors? Just as I supposedly prefer savanna, did early Homo sapiens prefer forest, where *they* evolved, to the savanna, where they eventually swooped down from the trees to walk? I wonder what other animals might share in this conundrum, which ones have dispersed all over the globe in a short amount of time relative to their evolution as a species. Cockroaches? Rats? Crows? Did these animals disperse only because of us—are humans creating a planet of homesickness?

Perhaps I should have listened to the snake whose body curled into a shape implying that what I stood before was endless—more ocean than lake. Even though giving in to the snake's deceit was what got us banished from the garden—our original home—in the first place, this was also the moment when we were most enticed by the land: conversing with its animal inhabitants, tasting its forbidden fruit, believing what it wanted us to believe. What I need is not to cease traveling, but to give in to temptation, to set aside my vigilance. I need to let myself be kidnapped by every place I visit, by this lake—to let it wash away my memory and see it as my first parent. Nature, after all—regardless of the desires of any gods her fauna create—selects more for opportunism than for loyalty.

I look back at the island as the ten-o'clock ferry pulls away. "Had enough?" one of the other campers had asked in the boathouse as we picked up our packs to leave, assuming we were going because of the rain. "No," we said. "This was all part of our plan." And it was. The island overwhelmed us, but she didn't make us flee.

This weekend, on the shores of Lake Michigan, I have learned that it is not "paper covers rock," this game we play with the land, but the game of memory. If a preference for savanna can take up residence in my genetic code for seventy thousand years, maybe my love of ocean comes from a memory much deeper even than that: some kind of molecular yearning for the sea vent or tidal pool where life began. It doesn't matter where I was born or where I grew up. I am indigenous to nothing. A lake can be an ocean. My allegiance can change; my genetic code a journal of shifting passions. I can love what I want. Perhaps this is our greatest myth: that there is somewhere we belong. And the skin we needed to shed was our entire idea of home.

METAMORPHIC

I am on all fours on the Lake Superior shore, ogling the contents of a pothole: pebbles and cobbles, water, and the sun's direct rays. Shirt sleeves rolled, I survey the colors—muted purples, greens, yellows, and blacks. I choose a stone, then reach in to retrieve it. So the process goes: like a god selecting souls, I compile a handful of stones, then move to the next pothole to see what it has to offer.

When we get home, my husband buys two field guides: *Is This an Agate?* and *Lake Superior Rocks & Minerals.* I've never been adept at identifying rocks. This granite we found—pink and speckled as a kestrel egg—is composed of quartz, mica, and feldspar. There is feldspar again in a pepper-colored rock I think might be diabase, but here the feldspar is mixed with augite and possibly hornblende, magnetite or olivine. You can see how things get complicated.

The difficulty goes deeper than simple composition. When identifying a rock, you often must detect the almost unfathomable process that melded its minerals together. Several of my rocks could be quartz or metamorphosed sandstone—quartz subjected to high temperatures and pressure, which would make them quartzite. The only difference, my field guide says, is that quartzite has a little more texture. Identifying rocks, it seems, is more about parts than wholes, more about process than product. It is less about naming what you've found than about understanding how that thing came to be. In this case, how volcanoes, glaciers, and plate tectonics, over billions of years, produced and changed the rocks I hold in my hand. And how ten thousand years of wave action in Lake Superior smoothed them into something I want to take with me.

With flowers, categorizing is a simple matching game: look at the flower, look at the field guide picture. Is it the same size, shape, and color? Even birds, which can disappear in an instant, aren't as perplexing to me as the rocks I can carry home to study with the aid of a library of reference books. Once, at a relative's cabin in northern Wisconsin, an odd bird landed on the deck seemingly just to confound us. Warbler-sized, the bird was a bright olive green with black wings and tail, blotches of white on its underside, and speckles and blotches of neon orange on its throat, head, and belly. It looked like a parakeet. But even without internet, and with only a few generic field guides dug out of a neighbor's basement, we identified it within three hours: a molting male scarlet tanager.

My understanding of rocks seems to go only as far as the broad divisions taught in grade school, and even on these categories I don't have a firm hold. So I look up definitions. Igneous rocks are basically cooled lava. Sedimentary rocks are compacted, cemented-together pieces of other broken-up rocks. And metamorphic rocks are rocks that have changed form. A University of Oregon website states: "Just as any person can be put into one of two main categories of human being, all rocks can be put into one of three fundamentally different types of rocks." Though the website clearly defines the rock types, it doesn't say anything about the two categories of human being, and I can't help thinking about the options that lie beyond the obvious divisions of male and female. Gay or straight? Accepted or marginalized? Convinced or uncertain?

＊

I like to roam the forest naming things. Wood anemone. Rue anemone. *False* rue anemone. I wonder what makes the third one false: its more deeply lobed leaves, its slightly smaller flowers? It's a buttercup, like the other two; but not, my *Newcomb's Wildflower Guide* indicates, an anemone.

When I was an environmental educator, I taught a class called Stone Wall Study. I hiked my mostly elementary-aged students to a wall—one with its upper boulders spilled in the sun, and gaps through which two could pass abreast— and asked them to speculate on the wall's original purpose, as well as to investigate the distinct habitats it now delineated. On one side was a red pine plantation; on the other, a mixed deciduous forest. *Which side of the wall looks more natural?* I would ask. *Did the wall keep something out or something in?* Once, during the class, I thought I had discovered a new species: on the wild side of the wall was what looked like an anemone with multiple tiers of petals, its flower a fancy petticoat, like some kind of double hybrid. When I couldn't find it in my books, I brought a local biology professor to check it out. Not a new species, he said, just an anemone with some kind of odd gene.

I don't know how well my students could imagine the farmer's sons who dutifully dug the rocks from the soil and piled them on the wall to provide safety for a few dairy cows, or the Civilian Conservation Corps crew that planted the red

pines in the deserted pasture one hundred years later. Even
with more life experience than my students, I myself have
trouble imagining what I can't see, and what has occurred
over a period of time longer than a lifespan. I am baffled by
the process that created the rock, known as Shawangunk conglomerate, of which this particular wall was composed. I've
always been plagued with a mental deficit for understanding
composition, processes, and change—the kind of thinking
the stones that I have brought home from Lake Superior also
demand—and this deficit has extended far beyond my ability
to properly identify our planet's rocky foundations.

All my life I've battled a sort of dyslexia of cause and effect.
On a recent canoe trip, I was mystified by a high browse
line on the trees overhanging a lake. *Did the deer stand in
the water and dine? How tall could the deer possibly be?* I wondered, until someone explained that in winter the lake froze,
and they walked across the ice to graze. A weirder example:
growing up in the early '80s, I lived for a while under the
fear that contracting AIDS turned you gay. My older sister
set me straight, telling me AIDS actually killed you. It didn't
make you gay; gay people got it. I was, initially, relieved: if I
contracted AIDS, I wouldn't turn gay, only die. (Now, older
and away from religious and family creeds, this response, of
course, is embarrassing.) But almost immediately a seemingly
darker worry surfaced: without a disease to cause homosexuality, how could I be sure to avoid this "affliction"? (For, at the
time, that is what I had gathered from society that homosexuality was.) "How do you know if you're gay?" I asked my
sister. The question arose from a presexual mind—one that
couldn't yet fathom romantic love or physical attraction to
anything. "You just wake up one morning and you know,"
was her response.

I couldn't understand how one day you would not know
and the next you would, so I imagined it must be like get-

ting your period—a milestone still many years off for me. I assumed you would open your eyes one morning and pull back the covers to reveal, on the bedsheets, written in blood, the universe's edict: gay or straight. I believed you had no say in the matter, that the issue was as tightly and long-ago cemented as a conglomerate's quartz and pebbles.

The issue, though, is much more complex. Some evidence does point to sexual orientation as something people awaken to—an inborn predisposition. Identical twins are more likely to both be homosexual than fraternal twins or non-twin siblings. And having several older biological brothers—whether you live with them or not—slightly increases a man's chance of being homosexual (from 3 percent to 5 percent), implying that the cause occurs prenatally. However, sexual orientation and sexual behavior are also considerably influenced by social and cultural factors. Among the Marind-Anim people of southern Papua New Guinea, teen boys freely engage in homosexual relations with each other and with older married men, whereas all women are presumed heterosexual. In ancient Greece, men in their twenties permissibly wooed boys whose beards had yet to grow.

Perhaps my childhood fears were influenced by a society focused too much on sex and not enough on love. As it turns out, recent research and theory indicate that human sexuality—especially women's—may harbor a subtle plasticity. Whether you fall into the category of heterosexual or homosexual, your sexuality may include a secondary characteristic that enables you to fall in love with people who contradict your sexual orientation. Regardless of any "odd" genes or environmental conditions (in womb or world) that may lead to one or another sexual orientation, love, it appears, is ultimately metamorphic.

✳

On the night of March 30, 1778, in Woodstock, Ireland, twenty-three-year-old Sarah Ponsonby donned men's clothing, grabbed a pistol and her little dog, Frisk, then climbed out the parlor window of the Georgian mansion where she lived with the family of her first cousin, Irish aristocrat William Fownes.

Twelve miles away, at Kilkenny Castle at ten that same night, thirty-nine-year-old Eleanor Butler, daughter of one of the period's most powerful Irish families, also put on men's clothing and secretly mounted a horse bound for Woodstock. Once there, she hid in a barn and waited for her dear friend. Avoiding unwanted marriages, they planned to travel twenty-three miles to Waterford, board a boat for England, and withdraw to the countryside to live together. Their escape did not succeed. The two women were returned to their families, who were relieved that the elopements did not involve men, which would have undermined the ladies' honor.

Sarah and Eleanor persisted, though, and openly now, in their desire to live together. Threatened with being sent to a convent, Eleanor escaped again, fled to the Ponsonby estate, snuck in through a hall window (aided by a housemaid), and hid in Sarah's closet. A day later she was discovered, but instead of coming to retrieve his daughter, Eleanor Butler's father sent word the two women could go away together. For ten days the Fownes family resisted, but when Sarah declared at all costs her one desire was "to live and die with Miss Butler," they too relented. Early on a May morning the two ladies left, with Sarah's housemaid, in a coach provided by the Butlers. Their journey ended in Llangollen, Wales, where they lived together for fifty years, studying literature and languages, writing letters and diaries, helping the poor, gardening, and running a small dairy. Despite keeping to themselves, they became widely known as "the ladies," and later "the Ladies of Llangollen."

For over a century, people have tried to identify what these two women *were*. Were they lesbians, or—as we so diminutively tend to put it—were they just friends?

*

Attempting to identify my rocks, I pause at a page in the field guide between Jasper and Laumontite titled Junk. It is structured the same as every other page, with a map depicting junk's occurrence along Lake Superior in the upper-right corner and the same headings, like Hardness and Streak, in the left margin. Next to Size the text reads, "Beach junk can be as small as a shard of glass or as large as furniture or appliances." Next to Where to Look the book says, "You can find beach junk all around the shores of Lake Superior." It's amusing to me that beach junk, though its name implies a lack of value, is important enough to have garnered a page in the guide, and that, although the idea of beach junk having a universal hardness or streak is ludicrous, an attempt has been made to mold such a find into the accepted classification system of rocks and minerals. But I'm confused by the accompanying picture, which shows a porcelain tile, beach glass, rusty metal, an aluminum blob, slag glass, and a piece of driftwood. How does driftwood—something natural, something people collect—fit into the same category as discarded furniture and appliances—basically trash? I suppose it's all about perspective. Like being "just friends" when you might be lovers, to a rock hound, even driftwood is junk.

Most scholars call the eighteenth-century relationship enjoyed by the Ladies of Llangollen "romantic friendship"—a particularly intense, exclusive, intimate, asexual love between same-sex friends (either male or female) that may or may not include holding hands, cuddling, kissing, cohabitating, and sharing a bed. Though the term "romantic friendship" did not come into use until the nineteenth century, passionate non-erotic friendships had already existed and been considered ordinary for some time: Plato describes them in his *Symposium,* circa 385 BCE; Montaigne describes them in his essay "Of Friendship," dated mid-sixteenth century. During Victorian times, romantic friendships flourished between middle- and upper-class women, likely because Victorian men and women—even married couples—resided in two opposing worlds, marriages were often arranged, divorce was rarely sanctioned, and women were assumed to be uninterested in sex. Thus, ardent female friendships—like the relationship between Eleanor Butler and Sarah Ponsonby—were tolerated and even encouraged.

These relationships have been tagged with all sorts of labels. Intimate friendships between college-aged women were termed "smashes" in nineteenth-century literature. "Boston marriage," another widely used phrase, originated in Henry James's novel *The Bostonians.* The phrase "mummy-baby friendships" comes from studies in Lesotho, South Africa, where intimate relationships between younger girls and slightly older girls are part of the female social order. Yet another name, "Tom-Dee relationships," is borrowed from Thailand; Tom is short for tomboy, and Dee for lady.

Even though contemporary America does have terms for intimate, nonsexual, same-sex relationships, such as "bromance" and "womance," it's hard for the modern American mind to understand and accept the concept. In the school where I teach, students titter at the way Brutus and Cassius speak of each other in *Julius Caesar,* throwing the words *love* and *lover* around shamelessly. According to Lillian Faderman, author of *Surpassing the Love of Men: Romantic Friendship and Love Between Women from the Renaissance to the Present,* society began scorning intimate same-sex friendships around 1920: "Such friendships are usually dismissed by attributing them to the facile sentimentality of other centuries, or by explaining them in neat terms such as 'lesbian,' meaning sexual proclivity. We have learned to deny such a depth of feeling toward anyone but a prospective or an actual mate."

As Faderman implies, everything today must be about sex. The idea of romantic friendship washes up on the shores of our post-Freudian era like so much beach junk, its field marks smoothed through the last century into something difficult to identify but simple to lump into a single, discriminatory category: latent homosexuality.

The lord's prayer of metamorphism goes like this: *limestone to marble, sandstone to quartzite, shale to slate, granite to gneiss.* I can recite it as if I am practicing for some kind of religious confirmation. But even as I utter the words, I don't really understand them. I remember the rock cycle. Igneous rock can become sedimentary or metamorphic. Sedimentary rock can become igneous or metamorphic. Metamorphic rock can become igneous, sedimentary, or even a new kind of metamorphic. But I am baffled by any description of how these processes actually work.

Limestone to marble, sandstone to quartzite, shale to slate, granite to gneiss. I recite the words again. At what point does the granite become gneiss? On what day? At what hour? That old dyslexia kicks in. Where is the line or the moment in time that divides what it once was and what it now is? Metamorphism, my source says, is impossible to observe; it can only be studied after some sort of weathering, erosion, or uplift. Often the processes that caused the change are tricky to discern. And metamorphism is not sudden; it takes millions of years for rocks to transform.

The changes that we suffer within ourselves can be just as incomprehensible. For a heterosexual, falling into a particularly intimate friendship with someone of the same sex (or, for a homosexual, someone of the opposite sex) can lead to a small crisis of identity when considered within the restrictive categories we currently use to describe relationships and sexuality. When Basil Hallward first saw Dorian in Oscar Wilde's *The Picture of Dorian Gray*, he stated, "I knew that I had come face to face with some one whose mere personality was so fascinating that, if I allowed it to do so, it would absorb my whole nature, my whole soul, my very art itself." I have met a woman like this.

She is where I have never been. She is almost always where I have never been. This time it is Biakpa, Ghana. Her husband is ill, in bed. She reads and looks for insects. She feeds grains of rice to three types of ant colonies, watches snails mate, finds a cigar-sized millipede. There are moths whose wings look like animal eyes or dead leaves, a green bug that looks like a green leaf, huge spiders, a caterpillar that hangs upside down from the ceiling with a tube that covers its body. Hard-skinned grubs stick to both the ceiling and the cement wall; their colors match what attracts them. She and the local kitty hunt in the evening. Where she crouches and looks, it crouches and looks, then it kills what she sees.

I know this because she has written me. In fact, what I have written above is almost entirely plagiarized—her version of herself, which she meant for only me to see. What I remember is her turning to laugh as she locked the cabin door before a hike during a three-day weekend in the woods, no husbands, in Michigan's Upper Peninsula. I was startled because I saw age in her face. The last time I had felt so close to a friend I was young. This woman was as old as my mother was then, and I am old enough to be my mother then, and neither of us are mothers—which is beside the point, but maybe it isn't. Inside us are half of each child we've never had and some small piece of all the women we've descended from. When I admire the distal edges of her fingernails, white and perfectly curved like the horizon of Ely, Minnesota, must have been the weekend she went mushing—which I read about on her travel blog (also there: a picture of her juggling with dried mud for some children along the Mekong River)—when I admire these things, it is because I love her passion for living.

One night, we are actually in the same place: full of seafood and wine, seated between our husbands at the musical *Wicked*. When the lovely Glinda, who becomes the Good Witch, sings to the emerald-green Elphaba, future Wicked Witch of the West, "Because I knew you, I've been changed for good," she whispers, "That's us!" and grabs my hand. I am taken by surprise. I whisper back, joking, "I guess I'm Elphaba." I say this because my friend is beautiful: hair the almost black of the basalt I brought home from the lake, eyes as blue as the kind of cloudless sky that almost everywhere, you must patiently await.

For one week, in the month of July, I go to where she is. To her favorite place on Earth: high desert, a place that's made of circumstantial evidence—dry riverbeds, already eroded buttes and mesas, a beauty mute and built on abstinence. She plans a ten-mile loop hike at Capitol Reef National Park, which sounds marine, but water is scarce here. We don't have four-wheel drive, so we have to hike five extra miles, round trip, to and from the trailhead. My husband comes along. Her husband stays back—at the end of our hike, he will meet us on the road, the blue plastic tub they use to wash their camp dishes filled with ice and a two-liter Diet Coke.

None of the dreams I had of hiking side-by-side, steeped in conversation, pan out because I hike much faster than she, especially on the uphills, which once or twice have made her faint. We hike to the lip of the waterpocket fold, a hundred-mile-long gash in the earth's crust, the rocks on one side lifted seven thousand feet higher than the other. It is dry, beautiful, alien. But by the end of the fifteen miles, I trail behind her and my husband, in so much pain I am crying. *It's because of the pounding,* she says. *These are not the soft soil trails of the forest. Everything is rock.*

She is where I would like to be. I do not mean she is there. I mean she is this thing: a sun-warmed rock next to a rushing stream—a rejuvenating combination of sunlight, stone, and water. When I travel, I seek out these things. Likewise, she is where my mind goes when it decides to wander.

Constant thought about the object of desire is a common sign of romantic love, as are a need for proximity and physical contact, despair at separation, elation when the object of desire gives you attention, and a tremendous awareness and understanding of the partner's moods. But in the article "What Does Sexual Orientation Orient?" Lisa Diamond points out that these feelings and behaviors also characterize the infant-caregiver bond. And who has not heard a new mother comment that she is totally "in love" with her child? Although we may not remember it, we were in love with our parents, too, during the first year or so of our lives.

The mistake most of us make is to assume romantic love evolved to ensure that mammalian mothers and fathers stuck together to raise their highly dependent young, and thus that it occurs in concert with sexual desire and is only legitimate when directed toward the opposite sex. But it's likely that romantic love between adults is what's known as an exaptation, a trait evolved for one reason but co-opted for something else. Here's why: from an evolutionary standpoint, long before there was "mating for life," there was the necessity for a mother to bond with her child—creating a totally physical, totally loving, but totally asexual relationship between her and either a daughter or son. The point here, as Lisa Diamond puts it, is that "romantic love and sexual desire are functionally independent," and "love knows no gender." In fact, humans may be biologically predisposed to experience romantic friendship.

The University of Oregon website that divided humanity into two undeniable (but unstated) groups gave this definition for metamorphism: rocks that have "moved into an environment in which the minerals which make up the rock become unstable and out of equilibrium with the new environmental conditions." So metamorphism is situation dependent. It's the process of adjusting to some kind of change, usually caused by increased temperature or pressure. Above 200 degrees Celsius (392 degrees Fahrenheit), rocks begin to recrystallize. Whatever elements are available in the original rock will break down and recombine in a different way, creating new minerals.

If temperatures reach 600°C, a complete meltdown occurs: rocks become magma, which, when cooled, creates igneous rocks, something entirely new. But during metamorphism, nothing is lost or added at the elemental level. The basic composition stays the same, which is what makes it so complex: the rock can still be what it is and yet be in the process of becoming something slightly different. What I don't get about metamorphism, that the metamorphism takes place while the rocks are in a solid state, is also perhaps what is so groundbreaking about new theories on human sexuality:

according to Lisa Diamond, it is possible for a person's sexual desire to change in the context of a single relationship, while that person's sexual orientation remains the same.

Diamond has coined the phrase "sexual fluidity" to describe this phenomenon. In her book by that name, Diamond addresses how most people believe the biological order of a romantic relationship entails sexual desire first (that initial "chemistry") and romantic love (the intimate bond) second. But, Diamond's research shows, the opposite can also be true, especially for women. What begins as an intimate friendship can turn sexual. Different from bisexuality, which involves regular attraction to both sexes, sexual fluidity might happen only once in a lifetime, or only a few times, or not at all. The likely catalyst is oxytocin, a hormone that facilitates not only bonding between infants and caregivers (or close friends) but also sexual arousability. Simply hanging out with someone you care deeply about can—sometimes and for some women—produce desires that conflict with a person's primary sexual orientation. In other words, the body's chemistry can temporarily change its own seemingly fixed tendencies. When this happens, the world may call you something different. But you are still you.

If you search Elizabeth Mavor's biography of the Ladies of Llangollen, or the diaries of the ladies themselves, you won't find a single hint of anything sexual. And neither will you here. All I can say is this: there is no field guide for love, or friendship, or the great variety of people one will encounter in a lifetime. Also: this is not a coming-out piece. It is about going inward.

One Christmas, we go with our husbands to Les Eyzies-de-Tayac, France. I want to see the engravings of early man, something inconceivably old. I arrange a visit to the Grotte de Bara-Bahau—an onomatopoeic name, given for the sound the large rocks that have fallen inside the cave must have made. We listen to a woman give a brief tour to just the four of us in broken English. We strain to see in the rock the living things she traces with her laser pointer: a reindeer, a horse without legs and a horse without a head, and aurochs—an early ancestor of cattle. The bear is a bit easier: natural convexities in the cave wall itself form its head and shoulders, a large flint pebble acts as eye, and from its mouth is etched a long line, representing the animal's breath. Easier still is the phallus, which my friend points out privately to her husband before the guide even gets to it, unsure if it is an actual engraving or an instance of pareidolia—the imagined perception of a pattern or meaning where it does not actually exist, like seeing a picture in the clouds. "Oh, yes," the guide chimes in, overhearing. "There is a phallus." This is rather rare; more common are depictions of female genitalia, I later read.

We leave the cave, joking like teenagers about my friend's singlehanded ability to identify the phallus in a cave of otherwise obscure engravings, but also about the strange question our guide repeated over and over during the tour, singling out each one of us, multiple times, as its recipient. "Do you *know?*" she would ask, the intonation and pronunciation of her mother tongue adding mystique to her inquiry. Then she would turn to the next one of us, making direct eye contact: "Do you *know?*"

"I do not know," she would respond to her own question. She seemed to want to preserve, in addition to the engravings, some other element of the cave's mystery.

❋

On the shore of Lake Superior, among those wave-carved potholes filled with stones, I looked in, chose the ones I liked, and held them close. But just as the page on beach junk in my field guide suggested, I also found something in one of those potholes that I didn't expect. When my husband accidentally dropped a coveted quartz pebble into the largest and deepest of the holes, I rolled up my shirt sleeve as far as it would go and leaned over to recover the stone. Suddenly, I saw myself.

It must have been similar to what Narcissus experienced in that silvery-surfaced forest pond. Never before had I seen a clearer picture than what I saw that day in the pothole. I couldn't move. Like Narcissus, all I could do was gaze. Perhaps what kept Narcissus at the pool, in admiration over what was before him, was not self-love but a fascination with the image of himself as reflected by the earth. What I saw in that pothole, now a portal, was not made of skin and bone—the usual "junk"—brown hair, brown eyes, small ears, my father's nose. I was made of water and stone. Though we may label ourselves heterosexual, bisexual, homosexual, lovers, or just friends, we should not be surprised to find that we are as dynamic as the earth that holds us up. We are simultaneously solid and fluid, inherently uncategorizable. We are always in the process of transformation.

Originally, life on Earth was divided into two kingdoms: plants and animals. Then there were three; then four; then five; now six. Perhaps two categories—whatever they may be—are not sufficient for humans either. Names that come from without are destined to be inaccurate. It is not what we are called that we must answer to, but what calls us from within.

THINK
LIKE A MOUNTAIN

"I wish I had my gun so I could shoot these pumpkins," Cody announced to his classmates before he even stepped off the bus. We were at the trailhead, next to a farmer's market and across the street from a pumpkin patch. We'd had a few frosts already, and with the vegetation blackened and flattened, the pumpkins were lined up like a rafter of turkeys.

"I'm in charge of the sack," Cody said next when I handed him one of two Camelbaks, each holding seventy ounces of water, which I planned to distribute in Dixie cups at the hike's midway point. We would hear the word "sack" over and over that morning, along with the fact that Cody was "in charge of it." I cringed each time. Cody was a master of sexual puns. If a word had even a hint of double meaning relating to intercourse or the involved body parts, he would find and exploit it. He was so good, in fact, that most of the other students didn't get his jokes.

"Everybody on your wood!" he shouted once, when I gave each student a square of paneling to mark where to stand during a team problem-solving activity. "I'm the giver, not the receiver," he made sure everyone knew, later in the game, when he was asked to hand something to someone.

But the problem with Cody wasn't his machismo or his hypersexuality. Many of the fifteen- and sixteen-year-old boys in my English class in the experiential, environmental program in Wisconsin where I taught for a few years suffered from these two hopefully temporary exaggerations of character. The students (all of whose names have been changed) who registered for the program—a multidisciplinary three-hour block class at a public high school—didn't do it because they were particularly concerned about global warming or because they had a strong environmental ethic. They signed up because they were the sons (and occasionally daughters) of farmers. They liked hunting, and they loved being outdoors.

Cody had been in my class the previous year, too, so I knew him well. And it wasn't his aforementioned machismo, or hypersexuality, or even his intolerance of homosexuality that I found surprising. No, what was so maddening about Cody was that he was all of these things and also one of the smartest students in the class. He was one of the few who'd actually read all of the *Adventures of Huckleberry Finn,* not just the first half of each chapter (the portion that could be finished in class). He and a partner had prepared an excellent translation and performance of the argument between Brutus and Cassius in their army tent on the battlefield after the assassination of Julius Caesar. I'd heard from another student that Cody, only a junior, had the highest grade in a senior chemistry class. Having Cody in class was always paradoxical. And when it came time to study the issue of wolves in Wisconsin, Cody embodied that paradox again. He would be both my biggest obstacle and most powerful tool in getting my students to realize there might be a valid way to view the wolf other than through the sights of a rifle.

＊

In his essay "Thinking Like a Mountain," Aldo Leopold admitted to once having just the kind of predator-mindedness that permeates the heads of Cody and many of my other male students. Leopold recounted a story about how he and a buddy once caught sight of a family of wolves in an open area beneath where the two friends stood on a cliff. "In those days," he wrote, "we had never heard of passing up a chance to kill a wolf. In a second we were pumping lead into the pack . . . when our rifles were empty, the old wolf was down, and a pup was dragging a leg into impassable slide-rocks."

At that time, Leopold viewed the wolf solely as a rival, a competitor in the hunt for deer. Cody shared this view. In preparation for studying Leopold's essay, I presented my students with a 2008 article about the reinstatement of wolves in Michigan, Minnesota, and Wisconsin to the federal endangered species list. They had been removed from the list just six months prior by the Bush administration, but the decision was overturned after a lawsuit from the Humane Society and several other groups. (Since that time, wolves in the Western Great Lakes region have been delisted and relisted multiple times, a pattern likely to continue ad infinitum.)

When I'd asked the students for their opinions, Cody hadn't responded in his usual, well-edited prose. Instead, he'd scrawled, "The wolfs should be killed. I have had it with these stupid bunny huggers wanting to see animals that shouldn't be there. They are just ruin[ing] the deer population."

Before settlers came to Wisconsin, there were an estimated three to five thousand wolves in the state. As hunters reduced the deer population, wolves found livestock to be easy prey. In 1865, a bounty of five dollars was offered for each wolf killed, to lessen losses for cattlemen. In 1900 the bounty was raised, but for a different reason: to ensure a good population of deer for hunters. At twenty dollars for adults and ten dollars for pups, it took just sixty years to extirpate wolves from the state.

In "Thinking Like a Mountain," Leopold describes how watching state after state extirpate its wolves—and how these extirpations affected vegetation and other wildlife—caused him to change his view of the wolf's role in nature. But "extirpate," which we came across in the news article, was a new word for my students.

"It means to make extinct from a local area," I explained.

"It sounds like constipated," Vince said from the back of the room. Vince, like Cody, always went for the laugh.

"Yes," I conceded, "it shares a suffix with constipated. But extirpated means that although there were no wolves in Wisconsin in 1960, they did exist elsewhere."

"In Alaska you can shoot wolves from an airplane!" exclaimed another flannel-shirt-wearing scholar named Brad.

"Really?" I asked, feigning interest. I had no idea what Brad was talking about, but it sounded made-up.

"Yeah," Cody said, excited by any talk of shooting wolves. "There's a $150 bounty on wolves in Alaska."

Later, I learned that Brad and Cody were right. Alaska allowed hunters to apply for permits to hunt wolves aerially in certain areas of the state where, on the snow-covered landscape, the wolves could be spotted almost as easily as pumpkins in a field after frost. I was impressed by my students' knowledge—at least, my two loudest students' knowledge—about the wolf situation in another state. But I knew we would soon be reading Leopold's "Thinking Like a Mountain." If the only thing that interested or excited my students about wolves was the prospect of killing them, how could I prepare them for Leopold's suggestion that the wolf has a role in nature other than to compete with humans for deer?

✳

The day that Cody declared his desire to shoot pumpkins, my colleague Glen and I had arranged for the students to hike a section of the Ice Age Trail, a national scenic trail that follows the farthest reach of the most recent glacier across Wisconsin. The students were studying glaciation in their social studies class, and in English we were putting together a newsletter for which they would write articles spotlighting this section of the trail. The hike was three miles—not long, but probably longer than most of the kids had walked. It was also rough terrain, with the trail running up and down numerous glacial features that we wanted the students to observe and write about.

We had decided to split the class in two and hike in opposite directions. On the bus, Glen looked over the class list and created two groups, expertly dividing up friends, enemies, and dating couples. He showed me the groups and told me to choose. I scanned the list, spotted Cody's name, and picked the group he wasn't in. But when Glen read the names aloud, he skipped over Cody's. He ended up on my hike. It didn't take Cody long to annoy me.

"Do you go to bars and get drunk?" he asked, sounding artificially loud and innocent.

"No, Cody, I don't," I replied, which was mostly true. (Except for the occasional birthday party, I don't go to bars and get drunk.)

He kept at it. "Do you go clubbing?"

The students giggled. "No, I don't go clubbing, Cody." The laughter continued, and we walked on.

I decided to take our mid-hike break at the top of a kame, which is basically a pile of sand and gravel. It's a place where meltwater pours through a hole in a glacier, and deposits its suspended load. Then, when the glacier melts away, it leaves behind a conical-shaped pile of glacial till—called a kame. Most kames are no more than one hundred feet high, and this one was less than that. Still, it was quite a hill for these students, who are used to walking no farther than they can drag a dead deer back to their truck in a much flatter part of Wisconsin.

When we reached the top, I asked who wanted some GORP, but no one knew what that meant. "Good Old Raisins and Peanuts," I explained, and they seemed pleased. It might have been the only thing some of them learned and remembered that day. Cody began dispensing water into his classmates' cups by squeezing the end of the tube protruding from the Camelbak. It's really meant to be used as a straw, so his classmates had to push against his back; eventually he just laid down on the ground to apply pressure to the sack in order to get the water out. The students talked as they ate and sipped their water, repeatedly going to Cody for refills. I heard one of the students say "keg," and then another say "shhhhh." They were joking about refilling their cups with beer.

I was worried about bringing up wolves in class again. I love Leopold's essay, but I wasn't sure I was ready for students like Cody and Brad to express their glee a second time at the prospect of killing wolves. With their deep voices and propensity to talk over others, they could make it seem like everyone in the classroom agreed with them. How could I get the students who believed that wolves should be on the endangered species list to speak out?

If certain students weren't going to put their perceived unpopular opinions out there, I decided I would do it anonymously for them. During my planning period, I pulled out their papers on the Wisconsin wolf article and reread their answers to the last question, which asked for their opinion on wolves as an endangered species. I chose twelve that were insightful and well argued—six for and six against—and typed them up, omitting the students' names. I planned to display them on the classroom's big screen. Then I tallied up all of the opinions and displayed the totals: ten were against putting Wisconsin wolves on the federal endangered species list, thirteen were for, and three were undecided.

"Oh God, are we talking about wolves again?" Brianna said as she entered the classroom. She glanced at Cody, who immediately looked up at the screen where I'd displayed the anonymous opinions. "I want to know who wrote the third one!" he yelled out, referring to a response arguing that wolves should be on the endangered species list because they are "a beautiful animal who, when they kill cattle, are just trying to survive."

I began the class by asking the students how many had heard a wolf howl. Two-thirds of their hands shot up, which surprised me, because I've never heard it myself —only a coyote. I explained we'd be reading Leopold's essay, and that he begins by describing what the howl of a wolf means to a deer, a spruce tree, a man, and a mountain. I played a ninety-second clip of a wolf chorus and asked the students to come up with an adjective to describe the howls or a phrase that explained what the howls reminded them of.

Half the class wouldn't keep quiet while I played the clip. Robbie thumbed through a magazine, looking at cars for sale and whispering to Brianna about Jeeps. Someone else howled along with the wolves. When it was over, Brad said the wolf's howl "reminds me it's time to go hunting," and Cody declared that the wolf's howl sounds "gay."

I gave each student three Post-it notes and a copy of the essay and then read "Thinking Like a Mountain" aloud.

When I got to the part about Leopold and his buddy "packing lead," I saw Brad smile and try to catch Cody's eye across the room, but Cody didn't seem to notice. He was focused on the essay. After the reading, I asked each student to come up with three questions to use in a small-group discussion.

Some of the questions dealt with vocabulary or minor details ("What is a rimrock?" "How can a steep downhill shot be hard to aim?"), but I was astonished by the depth of others. Two groups discussed the symbolism of the "green fire" that Leopold saw extinguished in the eyes of the old wolf he shot. Another tried to decipher the "secret opinion" Leopold says mountains hold about wolves. A third group tried to understand the quote, "He [who shoots wolves] has not learned to think like a mountain. Hence we have dust-bowls and rivers washing the future into the sea." My students wondered, "What does shooting wolves have to do with rivers?"

A few minutes later, I brought the students back together and asked several to share their questions. After the one about rivers, Cody raised his hand. I called on him. "Shooting wolves causes the deer population to increase," he began, in a descending monotone, as if nothing school presented him with could ever be difficult to unravel. "Then the deer browse the plants on the mountain, killing them. The roots of the plants are what hold the mountain together. So without wolves, eventually the mountain dies."

My eyes widened. Cody, hater of wolves and homophobic hunter of pumpkins and deer, had expertly understood and paraphrased Leopold's lesson. I raised my hands above my head, turned toward Cody, and began to bend in an "I'm not worthy" half-bow. Cody's face reddened, but I could see that he was happy. I worried for a moment that I might be crossing a line, that my motion could be misconstrued as something inappropriate, even sexual. But it was too late, and I was overcome with emotion—relief, gratitude, hope.

I wanted to make sure the whole class "got" the essay, so I asked for a volunteer to restate what Cody had said. Joe, a student who never misses a chance to tell me how much he hates reading, raised his hand and relayed, in his own words, the cycle that results from extirpating wolves: a brief increase in the deer population, an over-browsed landscape, erosion, and then a decrease in the deer population due to starvation. Bearing witness to this very cycle caused Leopold to change his own point of view, and I could only hope my own trigger-happy students might follow suit.

"Excellent!" I practically screamed, and then, borrowing one of the student's questions, I asked, "So what does it mean to think like a mountain?"

"The mountain is like a spectator!" a student called out.

"Mountains live a long time, so they see things," another yelled.

I stopped and stared toward the ceiling, my hands in a supplicating pose. "Am I dreaming?" I said aloud.

"Stop, you guys!" Kristen yelled from the back. "Or she's going to expect this all the time!"

There were only ten minutes left in class, and I had to get them started on their journal entries, because most of these kids don't do homework. If they didn't write about what it means to think like a mountain right away, they might never think about it again. I handed out the writing prompts, reminded them to write a full page, and pointed toward the clock.

But Cody, as usual, wasn't finished talking. I leaned down next to his desk and asked him to share his opinion with me quietly, so the other students could get their work done. After bantering back and forth about the status of deer in Wisconsin, Cody said this, referring to humans and wolves: "Look, we're talking about survival of the fittest here." I smiled. I liked the way he thought.

"I know. You're right," I said, tapping my nail beneath a line at the end of Leopold's essay, where he quotes Thoreau. "It all comes down to how much you believe in this statement: 'In wildness is the salvation of the world.'" I looked back up at Cody. "There are six billion humans on the planet. We may well be able to live," I continued, borrowing from scientist and essayist David Quammen, "on a planet of weeds—a planet without wolves, but with a lot of deer—and other animals that do well with the kinds of changes humans make in the environment. But sometimes those changes turn out to be not so good for us either."

※

I wasn't sure that Cody, or any of my other students, would be thinking like a mountain when I saw them again the next week. Who knew if they were even thinking like a mountain after reading the essay? Brad, after all, suggested "an ATV" when I asked them to write down what a hiker might want to bring on the Ice Age Trail.

But Glen told me he saw Cody talking to two girls next to his locker and stopped to ask the students what they thought of the trail. "It was awesome," Cody blurted out. Perhaps they will think not like mountains but like kames, at least some of the time.

I don't know how I feel about Wisconsin wolves being on the federal endangered species list. It seems that if a wolf is killing your cow or your poodle, you should be able to shoot it, as long as there is a sufficient population of wolves in the state. But what is a sufficient population of wolves when compared to a staggering population of humans? In 1836, the human population of Wisconsin was 11,836. (That figure does not include Native Americans.) Minimum estimates put the wolf population for that time at 3,000. But now there are 5.8 million humans in the state and just 905 wolves. The ratio of human to wolf has changed in the last 200 years, from 4 to 1 to 6,400 to 1. This, time and time again, is what we tend to forget: the human population on Earth is exorbitant. And what sector decides what we desire? Exactly how many wolves does a human need to survive?

"Zero," Cody might say.

But somewhere, in the back of his mind, the mountain may respond. "Only time will tell."

ENSKYMENT

I see the vultures immediately as we pass the junkyard and turn onto the spur of road that ascends steeply and circles around the cemetery to the doors of Patapsco United Methodist Church. It is the last Sunday of Advent in Finksburg, Maryland. Crammed into the extended cab of my father's compact pickup—he and my husband in front; my mother already at the service—with my legs sandwiched between the back of the passenger seat and my own chest, it is difficult to emerge. I pop out, landing beneath a large, leafless oak that rises above the steeple. My eyes travel up the trunk to the branches—each, it seems, adorned with a vulture. The birds bedeck the tree like dark ornaments ready to pilfer the church's yuletide hope.

"There must be seventy or eighty!" I exclaim.

"Yeah. They're always here," my father notes.

Despite the rain, I pull out my phone to snap a couple photos, then file into church for the worship service followed by the children's Christmas program, in which my nieces will be acting. When we leave, the vultures will still be there, overlooking the graveyard where, somewhere, lay two plots that will one day hold my parents. I will take more pictures, walking backward through the cemetery, my dress shoes sinking in the rain-wet earth, to get a better angle: the whole building, the whole venue of vultures. It's hard not to blame the weather on these birds: the drab sky a cloak they pull behind them wherever they go. The view at the church is laughable, almost embarrassing. We shrug our shoulders at it, this tree trimmed in truth, that awful scene in a nature film where you suddenly realize there is no protagonist.

The poet Robinson Jeffers once wrote of a vulture that circled above him while he rested on a hillside: "I was sorry to have disappointed him. To be eaten by that beak and become part of him, to share those wings and those eyes, what a sublime end of one's body, what an enskyment; what a life after death." Edward Abbey remarked that nourishing the wings of a vulture, for him, would be "immortality enough." Despite such wisdom, I know it is hardly satisfying this scavenger's rank appetite that the folks who fill these pews every week want for an afterlife, no matter how mystical the birds might appear as they soar, or how beautiful a word Jeffers has created to describe it. To me, the vultures in the oak on this rainy Sunday next to my parents' church appear like a fork in the road, a dichotomous key's two definitive choices: go to heaven, or become part of the food chain. It's a choice that churchgoing children everywhere face in a weirdly silent struggle and then, as adults, forget or suppress and pass down to their own progeny. I know this because of my own struggle, the struggle I see in my students, and how, on the other side now, I can't seem to properly pull them through.

As a high school English teacher, one year, during a mythology unit, I had my students journal about what they would say when their future children asked them how the earth was created. A couple shared their journals aloud in class.

"Jesus was juggling nine balls," read Cory, "and they fell into place and became the planets."

"The sun pooped out the earth," read Jack, "and then let go a big gas bubble that wrapped around the earth and became its atmosphere."

I was initially impressed with their creative humor until other students called them out, informing me that these ideas were copied from TV shows like *South Park*. But then, as often happens in the classroom amidst the antics and swagger, like a single feather suddenly coming to rest, a sober thought unveiled.

"What I never understood," interrupted Kent, as he walked along the back wall of the classroom for no apparent reason, "is how God made the earth first, and *then* humans, and *then* animals, but the dinosaurs went extinct *before* we were around."

The feather that fell came to rest between the students and me, and everyone waited to see which way my response would send it. I understood where Kent was coming from. I would hardly identify my—or his—family as fundamentalist or creationist. This is not the Bible Belt; I teach in Stevens Point, Wisconsin, which is primarily Catholic, Lutheran, and Evangelical Lutheran, all of which have officially sanctioned the theory of evolution. Regardless, I, like Kent, was brought up to believe in the literal six-day creation of Earth as it was laid out in Genesis. But when I arrived at school, I learned about conflicting things: the big bang, plate tectonics, natural selection. It was almost as if these stories—the history of the earth and its people that I learned in church, and the history of the earth and its people that I learned in school—were really about two different planets, and I had to choose which one to inhabit. I couldn't answer Kent's question. I paused, wrestling with my thoughts. I knew what my answer would be if I spoke. Was I afraid of being accused of intolerance? Or actually *being* intolerant? Or did I just not want to be the bearer of bad news? It's easy to tell a child he's descended from a common organism, along with all other life on the planet, but I knew where this knowledge would lead. How do you tell a child when he dies, that's it? So I did what seemed less cruel: asked him to sit down and proceeded with the lesson, leaving him in the same no-man's-land between church and school that I, too, had navigated alone thirty years ago.

When I was a child, my father's aunt, who was a Jehovah's Witness, gave me a copy of *My Book of Bible Stories.* I loved this regal book, its title in shiny red calligraphy on a gold cover, its all-color, realistic pictures stretching a full or half page. I remember the picture before the great flood, when giants inhabited the earth: on an orchard path stood two hulk-like men with trim hair and beards, impressive pectorals, and bulky biceps. In a single hand, one held a young man by the neck near the top of a tree overflowing with coconuts; the other stole a basket of fruit from a small, distressed family— several grapes and a single tomato were falling to the ground. I remember the picture of Jonah, suspended in white wisps of disturbed water, looking rather squid-like: green seaweed encircled his head and flailed out from it like many arms; his robe ballooned around his waist. Beneath him waited a blocky whale, its linear lower jaw already open.

The picture I remember most, though, is a picture of the destruction of Sodom. In it, fireballs came from the sky, Sodom burned in the distance, and a man and two women, frightened and upset, were running out of the illustration.

But Lot's wife, who had turned around against God's wishes for one last look at her home, had become a pillar of salt. "Can you see her in the picture?" the text asked. How could you not? It was quite alarming for a children's book. Fixed to a small patch of barren ground, green hills to the right, burning city to the left, her body turned, arms outstretched, she looked as if a thick layer of plaster of Paris had been poured over her—and only her—head.

But more alarming than the picture of Lot's wife was the book's first line: "THIS is a book of true stories," it read. "The stories give you a history of the world from when God began to create until right up to our present day. . . . The stories appear in the order that events occurred in history."

I already knew the stories the book contained. They had been imparted to me over the years in the half-underground Sunday school rooms of Patapsco United Methodist. While I don't remember anyone there making an assertion of truth as strong as the one in *My Book of Bible Stories,* I don't remember anyone ever suggesting these stories were metaphors either. This is in keeping with one study that labels religious talk a special type of communication called "denied metaphor." Unlike the metaphors abundant in regular speech, whose metaphorical value is acknowledged, religious metaphors are claimed to be true. Such claims, the researchers argue, ensure your membership in a cooperating group, be it Christian, Buddhist, Hindu, or any of the other thousands of religions that exist in the world. By suspending skepticism and repeating the supernatural claims others make, you reap the charity and protection the group affords. You are considered a trustworthy affiliate of the community—or even kin, as religious terminology often intimates, replete as it is with the usage of father, mother, child, sister, and brother. Religion, accordingly, is a direct avenue to what evolutionary biologists call reciprocal altruism, a sort of I-help-you-now-you-help-me-in-the-future mentality, usually applied only to immediate relatives. Religion allows you to extend your idea of who is family.

So, in those tiny red-carpeted rooms of the Methodist church, with their chalkboards and pencils and paper and tables surrounded by yellow maple chairs that grew successively larger as I advanced through each class, I listened as adults in my community—a hairdresser, a music teacher— told me how snakes spoke, seas parted on command, the sun stood still, and a man walked on water and turned fishes into loaves.

According to the Pew Research Center's Religion and Public Life project, in 2008, the United Methodist Church wrote a resolution stating that the theory of evolution does not conflict with the church's teachings, that the creation story in the Bible, meant to teach religious principles, is metaphorical, not scientific. While creationism and intelligent design might hold a place in religious classes, they wrote, the two did not belong in science curricula. But a 2011 Gallup poll reports that 54 percent of those who attend church weekly—which I did with my family while growing up—are biblical literalists. In 2017, Gallup reported the numbers of biblical literalists were dropping; still, 35 percent of Protestants, 21 percent of Catholics, and 7 percent of those reporting no religion maintained that the Bible was the actual word of God and should be taken literally. The National Center for Science Education, in a 2004 article titled "The Creationists: How Many, Who, and Where?" call the focus of their study a "morbid condition" and later a "disability." They refer to the subjects of their study as "those afflicted." On the one hand, they note that biblical literalism could be caused by a deficit of knowledge, but on the other, they go so far as to call it a "disease of the intellect."

✳

Vultures were once thought to spread disease. They pick at decaying carcasses' natural orifices—like the eyes and anus—to gain entry, sink their bald heads deep to feed, vomit in self-defense, and regularly urinate and defecate on their own legs.

But, as signified by their scientific family name—*Cathartes,* which means "purge" or "purify"—we now know they do the opposite: rid the earth of disease-infested remains that could make other animals sick. Highly acidic enzymes in the vulture's stomach kill many of the diseases they eat, such as anthrax and hog cholera, as well as salmonella and botulism. Their lack of headdress makes for a clean exit when feeding, preventing diseased material from collecting there and being spread elsewhere. Ditto for their feet: urohidrosis, or cooling themselves with their own urine, probably acts doubly as a disinfectant, washing away any bacteria from their scaly legs with antibiotic digestive juices. A single vulture will scan over eleven thousand acres for food, making its cleansing efforts far reaching. Vultures don't spread death and disease but eliminate it.

So much a symbol of vigor is the black vulture in Columbia, cancer patients cook and eat the bird as an alternative treatment, sprinkling a powder made of dried meat and pulverized bones over food and beverages, draining and drinking the blood mixed with berry juice or wine. Though the hope is not for eternal life but merely to avoid a shortened one, I can't help but be reminded of the sacrament of communion. How many times had I knelt at the altar in the building over which these vultures now roosted, swallowed a chunk of homemade bread baked that morning by one of the church ladies, then threw back a half-ounce of grape juice like a watered down, flavored dose of medicine? I knew what the antidote was for, but I strained to comprehend just how it worked.

The vulture has actually been associated with the Virgin Mary. Several early cultures believed all vultures were female and that they were impregnated by wind—perhaps due to the vulture's habit of nesting high in cliff tops, where mating behavior might not have been observed. In the fourth century AD, St. Ambrose of Milan used vultures as proof of what I had returned to my parents' church in Maryland to celebrate with my family but at some point had turned away from believing: the virgin birth. He wrote, "Is that thing thought impossible in the Mother of God which is not denied to be possible in vultures?" The presence of vultures at the church had at first seemed ironic, a stark contrast to what was going on beneath them inside that steepled building, but their message was now more complex, more difficult to digest: maybe to rid myself of infirmity, to ensure my place in eternity, instead of bread and grape juice, all those years I should have been gnawing on a leg or wing or drinking the blood of a vulture.

Early on, I used to sit in church each Sunday half expecting the doors to open and Jesus to walk in. I was told he was going to come again, and I believed it, and thought he would pick a church as unassuming as ours to appear in. I wore angel wings, bordered with gold Christmas tree garland and roped to my torso, in many a Christmas program. I was even Mary once. My mother showed me how to kneel with my arms crossed, each palm near the opposite shoulder, like the figurine in our nativity at home. But it was the gaze I worked on hardest. Beneath my mantel, made from a blanket or bedsheet, I was locked into position, eyes fixed on whatever doll we were using as a stand-in for Jesus. "She never moved," my grandmother kept repeating after the program. "She never moved."

But Jesus never came. Every year, though, on the evening of the last Sunday of Advent, after the children's Christmas program, there would be a jingle of bells, the double doors at the back of the church would fly open, and—I kid you not—Santa would walk in to give us all a paper cup of candy and an orange.

In addition to his appearance at my church, I could see Santa in the little house outside of Woolworth's every December. He gave me candy canes and a coloring book. I sat on his lap, two solid thighs in a thick pantsuit. Every year he deposited under the tree of my frugal parents—perhaps the most incredulous miracle of all—an unimaginable amount of wrapped toys. But even with Santa, who was so tangible, there were questions. *How did he enter our chimney-less house? How did he make it all the way around the world in a single night?* I still remember in second grade, getting ready for school and asking my mother if Santa was real; in response, she used an odd, old metaphor, one I hadn't heard before but understood quite well: "Do you want me to burst your bubble?" she said. When *that* came out as a charade, what was I to make of David surviving the lions' den, Sarah giving birth at age ninety, stories already more insubstantial than anything I thought I knew of Santa? How on earth could I believe them? Santa just complicated an already difficult menu.

There was no parallel moment—no bubble burst—in regard to religion. The severing of my belief in the stories of the Bible, from Methuselah's age to the burning bush to the virgin birth and the resurrection, wasn't quick, but more like the slow splintering of a bough weighted down by ice or snow and that never rose again. There came no sudden snap of disconnection, the kind you listen for when gathering kindling for a fire. Instead, my belief frayed; it split by degrees, over a long period.

As a senior in high school, in a crowded hallway of kids changing classes, I once asked my own English teacher the same kind of question that Kent asked me. Both Twain expert and assistant football coach, this man had a large following. He had long black-and-silver hair that he sometimes pulled back in a ponytail. He wore sport sandals with his khakis so that we stared at his bare feet while he taught us transformational grammar instead of the traditional kind. Did he think there was a God? I asked him. What did he believe would happen when he died? "No" and "nothing" were his responses.

The debate was still going on in college, though by then I had become less blunt, more of a listener taking in knowledge. I savored the words of one man, tall and bald, my biology professor and colleague at an environmental education center where we worked. He laid bare every bit of knowledge possible about the natural world: when a specific wild hepatica flower was going to sprout each spring next to a rock behind the dining hall; where a pair of flying squirrels was nesting in an electrical box near the dormitory; why the pine vole was monogamous and the meadow vole was polygamous; how the mind of man had invented God.

The last I heard, the English teacher married a Christian woman and became a Promise Keeper, part of a group that, according to their website, "is on a mission to strengthen and equip every man to live with integrity and be a changemaker for Christ." The biology professor divorced and fell in love again. He recently wrote me: "Although still a staunch atheist, old age has softened my existential stance—I find myself thinking more and more about 'meaning,' something I would have never entertained in years past. . . ."

I don't know what I'm supposed to make of these changed points of view in my former teachers, people I assumed had it all figured out. That women are the real purveyors of religion? That a man's most central and stoic philosophy can be altered by love (or sex)? Or maybe this: religion is like a pebble dropped into the world next to us when we are born, whose ripple will pass through our minds for the rest of our lives, its amplitude and frequency changing, but never completely dying.

※

Vultures, my mother says, like to hang out in cemeteries. I don't believe her.

"So-and-so looked it up," she argues, so I do too.

And it's true.

A quick internet search reveals numerous articles about cemeteries in multiple cities that have, at one time or another, had a vulture problem: the Cedar Hill Cemetery in Vicksburg, Mississippi; the Graceland Cemetery in Mayville, Wisconsin; even the historic Gettysburg Battlefield reports a population of nine hundred vultures that have been residents for 150 years. Is it because they can—well—smell the dead?

North America's resident vultures, the black vulture and the turkey vulture, lie at opposite ends of the olfactory spectrum. Black vultures, like old-world vultures and most birds in general, are known for their poor sense of smell, but turkey vultures have one of the largest olfactory bulbs of any in the avian species. In experiments, turkey vultures ignored visual bait when no odor was present and were attracted to odor cues without visual bait. But the age of the carcass—and hence the strength and flavor of the smell—also influenced their feeding activity. In captivity, turkey vultures much preferred fresh-killed chicks over decaying food, and in the wild, one-day-old carcasses attracted a greater number of turkey vultures than either fresh or four-day-old meat. Rancid carcasses were completely ignored.

The moral? Vultures like cemeteries not *because of* your deceased grandmother but for the same reason you put her there yourself: the large beautiful trees, and the peace and quiet. It's a fitting place for them both—Grandma can wait patiently for her body to be resurrected after Christ's Second Coming and joined with her spirit in heaven. High in a tree, the vulture can roost undisturbed through the night, where in the morning it will spread its wings to warm and disinfect them with the ultraviolet light of the sun, then fly off to scan the streets for roadkill.

Once, I read aloud an Iroquois creation myth to my eleventh graders. "Long before the world was created there was an island floating in the sky, upon which the Sky People lived," I read. "They lived quietly and happily. No one ever died or was born or experienced sadness. However, one day one of the Sky Women realized she was going to give birth to twins. She told her husband, who flew into a rage."

"That doesn't make sense!" yelled an angry voice from the middle of the room. It was Clara—her mode of communication usually consisted of calling out, whether she was angry or not, but at this moment she did seem frustrated, adamant.

"What do you mean?" I asked.

"It says that when they lived no one ever died or was born, but then in the next sentence one of the Sky Women realized she was going to give birth. It just said no one was ever born. It's contradictory." She looked at me pointedly, ready for a challenge.

In spite of her predictable manner, I was surprised by the interruption and so, I think, were the other students. None of us was bothered by such a sudden plot turn in a myth from another culture—after all, *we* didn't believe it. But she was reading the myth differently, trying to see it through the eyes of the people who may have taken it for truth. Standing there in front of the room, deciding how to deal with Clara's concerns and continue with the lesson, I remembered what Clara had written in her journal: *I will tell my future children that the world was created in six days, as the Bible says, by God and no other. I do not believe in evolution and can't imagine that humans have descended from apes.*

I had read her entry with restrained fury. I made no marks on it; after all, it was a journal and I had asked for an opinion. A teacher must remain unbiased. But I had asked her what she *would* say, not what she *wouldn't* say. And wasn't this just more evidence of American schools lagging behind in science? In a 2015 Pew Research survey, only 65 percent of Americans stated that they believe in evolution, and over a third of those (24 percent of all Americans) believed a supreme being guided that evolution. In European countries such as Denmark, Sweden, France, and the United Kingdom, closer to 80 percent believe in evolution by natural selection. Wasn't a teacher supposed to correct, as the National Center for Science Education calls it, deficits of knowledge?

Today, in class, I felt that ire again. Should I burst *her* bubble, settle things for her in a single moment, give her the clean break I had never had? It wasn't until college, sitting in a senior seminar called Evil in Literature, studying the fall of man in Genesis, that I noticed the paradoxes in my own creation story. In Genesis, chapter 1, God creates man and woman last, both in his image, with no mention of dust or ribs. But in Genesis, chapter 2, God creates the heavens and the earth, *then* man, *then* all the plants and animals. It's not until later, when Adam gets lonely because he can't find an animal like him, that God puts Adam into a deep sleep and creates woman out of his rib. I was angered that more hadn't been made of the first story in my upbringing, the one where Adam and Eve seemed equal. *So which is it?* I wanted to ask Clara now. How is that any less contradictory than Sky Woman giving birth in a land where no one had ever given birth before?

Clara isn't alone in her bewilderment by the seeming absurdity of religious myths one didn't grow up with. When early European anthropologists first began studying what they labeled totemism, they couldn't make sense of how the Australian aborigines, when questioned about their beliefs, undeniably claimed that they, themselves, *were* kangaroos or witchety grubs or blackbirds. How could one believe such a thing? But what I can't understand is the European anthropologists. Why is the Christian God allowed to have plot discrepancies, failures of suspension of disbelief—in short, to do weird things—but not everyone else's?

I could have posed this question—an honest question of my own—to Clara and her classmates. But this could be considered denigrating to her religion, which, I am well aware, is not kosher in the classroom. I feel I've failed on two counts. What I want to know is this: how do you teach the truth? And how do you teach a myth?

※

Sometimes, the truth is frustratingly forgettable. Most of us have used mnemonic devices in order to ace one elementary-school test or another. For example: My Very Excellent Mother Just Served Us Nine Pizzas—or, now that Pluto has been demoted, Nachos. Here's a new one that seems pertinent here: Mary's Virgin Explanation Makes Joseph Suspect Upstairs Neighbor. It can be tough to recall lists of facts, like the order of planets in our solar system, unless we link them in a silly sentence.

Religious myths, however, easily grace our memory. Most memories degrade over time; those that don't are termed resilient. A study by anthropologist Scott Atran and psychologist Ara Norenzayan has shown the most resilient memories are not things that could actually happen (whether ordinary or uncommon) or things that are completely nonsensical, but stories that are minimally counterintuitive—that is, mostly realistic with just one or two supernatural events. When given "belief sets" consisting of multiple two- and three-word phrases, adults in their study had the lowest rate of memory degradation over time for sets of mostly intuitive statements mixed with a few phrases that were minimally counterintuitive. This means they could remember sets such as *crumbling ice, gossiping child, wandering deer,* and *sobbing oak* much more accurately after three months than any other combination of statements. A little bit of counterintuition, it seems, like the sobbing oak, gives stories a "mnemonic advantage," helping us remember even the intuitive portions. And this, the researchers note, is just what folktales and religious narratives are like; they make sense but amaze, feel both familiar and marvelous. We seem to have a cognitive template for myths. We remember them easily and well, then pass them down intact from generation to generation.

But this, of course, is only half the story. My real quest is how we can believe in such stories, not just why they get stuck in our heads. Cognitive psychologist Steven Pinker offers a simple answer. In addition to the fraternity they offer, and their innate memorability, these stories wrestle with real problems—like our impending death. If what we want is consolation, they won't offer that as fiction, only as fact.

I can't stop repeating the minimally counterintuitive statements from Atran and Norenzayan's study. *Admiring frog. Giggling seaweed. Sobbing oak. Melting grandfather.* They remind me of the mnemonics I offer my husband each time we leave our car at the airport parking garage when flying out to visit my parents. As we wheel our bags along the pedestrian pathway, I'll turn back and look for the writing on the wall: a number, a color, a letter. Knowing I'll never remember these hard facts of the parking map key, I'll say to my husband, aloud, "thirteen yellow bullets," or "seven red feet," or "nine blue ghosts." The phrases will slip away then reappear a week or so from now when, tired from my journey and ready to get home, I need them most.

I want to know whether the roost of vultures outside of Patapsco United Methodist consists of black vultures or turkey vultures, the only two vultures in North America. For some reason, it's important to me to know exactly what they are. In their breeding season, turkey vultures are widespread across the continental United States. Black vultures have only in the last sixty years or so moved north, through the Mid-Atlantic States and into New England. I scrutinize the photos we took while visiting, but I can't discern the color of the heads (red would mean turkey vultures, although they don't develop this blush until they're mature), nor can tell I tell their relative size (turkey vultures are bigger), nor the shape of their tails (black vultures' are more blunt). I email my mother.

"We think they are turkey vultures but are not really sure," she writes. "We are going to start riding around the church taking our bird book with us so we can check them out." I think about the bird book I gave my parents as a Christmas gift years ago, along with a bluebird box or hummingbird feeder. I had taken an ornithology class and wanted my parents to know what birds alit on their porch railing and bathed in the birdbath my mother has faithfully filled with water for the last forty years. I found it a pleasure to name them, as it must have been for Adam when God brought him every fowl of the air and beast of the field to see what he would call them. The bird book sits on the same living room shelf as *My Book of Bible Stories,* which describes Adam's naming spree in chapter three. Apparently, my efforts have not been fruitless. My mother notes: "We do refer to that bird book you gave us when we see something we want to identify."

Every year I assign my students a research paper, and once, two girls in my senior English class, inspired by an article in *Time,* explored whether it was possible to believe in both God *and* evolution. I stayed after class one overcast Thursday to help the girls with their outlines. Jamie described how she once challenged a counselor at Bible camp who was telling her cabin of eleven- and twelve-year-olds a story about a man who was swallowed by a whale.

"Jonah?" I asked.

"Yeah, Jonah!" Jamie responded. She explained that she raised her hand and said, "That didn't really happen. You couldn't survive in the belly of a whale."

"Its stomach acids would kill you," her friend chimed in, still reasoning out the story. (And so must I. She's right—if you even made it far enough to see the stomach acids. The only whale with a gullet large enough to fit a human—the sperm whale—has jaws lined with functional eight-inch teeth. The acid-less first stomach of the sperm whale uses muscular walls to crush its prey—usually giant squid. If you did somehow make it to the digestive acids in the second stomach, you would likely have suffocated already from the lack of oxygen. And any whale with ill intentions is probably just going to hammer you dead with its powerful flukes in the first place, rather than consume you.)

The counselor, though, Jamie said, asked if she was implying that the story wasn't true. It was at this moment that Jamie realized you didn't debate this stuff in church. At least not in her church.

I helped the girls organize their notes, but the conversation strayed. Both struggled with the lack of empirical truth in religious stories, yet both saw the need for religion in their lives. I held back, as I was wont to do, letting the girls draw their own conclusions. But I was thinking about what myth expert Joseph Campbell had to say on this subject. Writing in *The Inner Reaches of Outer Space* about the Judeo-Christian concept of a physical heaven, an actual place where resurrected Christians will spend eternity, Campbell articulates exactly what my students were experiencing. "What, in the name of reason or truth, is a modern mind to make of such evident nonsense?" Campbell asks. He goes on to advise, "Every myth, that is to say, whether or not by intention, is psychologically symbolic. Its narratives and images are to be read, therefore, not literally, but as metaphors."

For once, I decided to break the silence. The school day, after all, was technically over. I passed Campbell's sentiments along to my two students, saying what I wished I had been told outright at some point in my youth: I carefully stated that perhaps the truth in religious stories lay not in the narratives but in the themes, in the lessons the stories held about how to live a full and moral life.

Afterward, I worried I'd said too much, that my principal would call me down after a parent phoned in a complaint, but instead I got an eerie, unexpected, and immediate response: the room darkened and it began to pour, one of those sudden onsets of heavy rain that reaches through the steel and concrete of modern buildings and plays at your ears like the sound of your own blood through your veins in the moment before you faint.

"Is that rain?" Jamie asked.

"Maybe God's angry because we're talking about evolution," I quickly said, and we all laughed, relieved, I think, that I didn't expel God altogether from my nearly empty classroom.

✳

Throughout our visit, my husband took several photos of the vultures at the church. At the airport, waiting for our plane, he set one of the images as the background on his phone; later, at home, when I sat down to work at our computer, I saw he had made one of the images the wallpaper there as well. We're mesmerized by the pictures: the vultures and the church bell sit opposite one another in the sky, in nearly the same plane, hunched black shoulders and curved bronze chamber seeming to square off in some sort of silent match, absent of clanging or guttural grunts, anything that might hint at who was fighting or over what.

Their presence at the church is unnerving, to say the least, like the opening of a bad horror flick. But mythologically, the vulture isn't always portentous of doom. Many, aware of the bird's excellent vision, believed it had powers of clairvoyance. So it seemed to the Greeks and Romans, who noted how it frequently followed them into battle. In ancient Egypt, the mother goddess Nekhbet was often depicted in the form of a vulture; as mother of the pharaoh, she offered protection and rebirth. And many have heard of the Parsi, of the Zoroastrian faith, famous for their practice of laying out the dead in special towers to be consumed by vultures. Incidentally, this cultural practice has been threatened by the decline of vultures in India due to poisoning by the painkiller Diclofenac, often given to dying cattle and buffalos—which Hindus will not kill for religious reasons—to relieve their suffering. Diclofenac, banned in 2006 for use in animals, causes the vultures' kidneys to fail; it brought three species of South Asian vultures to near extinction. There were still crows and kites to scavenge the bodies of the Parsi's loved ones, but they took weeks to remove the flesh, unlike a group of vultures, which did the job in mere hours.

I think about the vulture's own viewpoint, how things must look from his roost at the church. The oak he sits in likely doesn't branch but conjoins, an infinite choice of perches fusing into one grooved trunk. The bridge, the streets, the railroad tracks, the spur of road that encircles his roost must seem a useless alphabet dropped on the earth. Junk cars probably gleam the same as the metal roof of the church. Stones, some square, jut up in rows, as designless as the hill's jagged nose. This is what he knows: each post of a fence that seems absurd (how easily he crosses it) holds exactly one bird; nightly, his wake settles in the oak; sun warms; carrion too. Without words, nothing is legendary; the myths he engenders elude him.

I'm excited to see my nieces perform in the Christmas program, though it turns out I will only see one of them, because the other is ill and at home. My sister plans to step in for her absent daughter, the thought of which makes me giggle, but in the end another adult acts as understudy. The number of children that attend our church has dwindled, so my little niece is both Gabriel and Mary. Today, the setting of the play is a children's nursery, where the younger children act out the nativity with their toys—a hobby horse, a baby doll—while the older children read the story. Jesus makes his appearance only briefly, held above the communion rail in two hands like a recently unwrapped present raised dutifully before a parent with a camera. Then the kids line up and play a few tunes as a group with handbells: "Away in a Manger," and "We Wish You a Merry Christmas."

I know what is coming next. It was listed in the newsletter mailed to me in Wisconsin (I'm still on the books as a church member) under "2013 Coming Events," next to December 15, the original date of the children's program before it was snowed out. "Children's Christmas Program during church service" the newsletter read, "with a special visitor." Accordingly, Santa walks in.

He walks toward the sanctuary and steps up into the chancel area. The chair to the left of the altar is pulled to the side and offered to him; his pants blend with the fabric and color of the seat cushion. My sister and her daughter exchange whispers. Then my sister leans toward me and says, her eyes wide with complicity, "It's the real one this year! Last year they said it wasn't the real Santa." Ever confused, I nod anyway.

Later, at home after lunch, when the family has gathered in the living room, my mother will say, "Santa did a good job this year, didn't he?"

And I'll blurt out: "Yeah, who was it?"

"Santa!" My mother will respond without skipping a beat, leaning forward, flashing at me those same wide eyes I saw an hour ago on my sister.

I feel embarrassed, and I change the subject quickly. My niece, who has paused, goes back to playing. Why am I so poor at this game? I think about a moment last summer, when my older niece was discussing how she was made by her mother, and her mother was made by her grandmother, and so on down the line.

"Yes," my mother interjected. "And we're all descended from Eve."

I made some brief comment about evolution. My mother, across the room, just shook her head at me with a little smile. Sometimes, it feels more wrong to be a scrooge than an atheist.

＊

"The eye that mocks a father and scorns to obey a mother," according to Proverbs 30:17, "will be eaten by the vultures." In contrast to St. Ambrose, many of the references to vultures in the Bible are negative. But my mother tells me the man who hands out the bulletins every Sunday has begun to call the wake of vultures "our friends."

"He brings them up EVERY week," she writes me in an email. "He counts them and lets us know what trees he sees them in. Right after you left here I went up there for something and every fence post had a buzzard on it. They were on the ground in front and back of the fence and down the hill beyond the fence. It is such a sight to see them lined up on that fence. I think I counted over seventy of them that day. Some had their wings spread and others didn't. It sometimes makes me think of that Alfred Hitchcock movie, *The Birds*. It is eerie when you are by yourself. It is almost like an omen."

Then, in closing, she has typed, "Have to go. *The Big Bang Theory* is on!"

The irony of her last phrase is not lost on me. I wonder if she believes in the big bang, so in an email I present her with the United Methodist Church's resolution on evolution. *Maybe you already knew this,* I write. She responds that she does believe the science and knows the religious stories are metaphors, but that both only answer so many questions and require their own sort of faith. I'm not satisfied—but not because of what she's written. It's because of what I've asked.

I've missed the real question. We can waste all our time arguing about the big bang theory and evolution's compatibility with religion. The problem though, comes not when we think about our origins, but rather when we consider where we are going. What if I asked my students to journal about what they think will happen when their lives end? What if I asked my mother? I believe there's *something,* is the response you'll get from many, religious or not, for the sole reason that the other option—that there's *nothing*—is as unimaginable as it is unbearable.

Like Lot's wife, I am unable to avoid the temptation to look back where I came from. Copper serpent, talking donkey, golden calf—the minimally counterintuitive titles of the tales in *My Book of Bible Stories* seem always to be just beneath my mind's surface. Imprinted in my brain is the book's last color picture. In it, a blue stream flows past two trees dressed in autumn-colored leaves toward mountains full of snow. Red and white flowers bloom in a bed lined with river stones. It seems to be all the seasons at once. An African American boy is feeding a spotted fawn. A little Caucasian girl is on her knees, petting a lion cub. Delighted adults watch the children. "Look at those tall trees, pretty flowers, and white mountains," the book reads. "See how the deer is eating out of the little boy's hand. And look at the lions and the horses standing over there in the meadow. Wouldn't you like to live in a house in a place like this?" As a child, I couldn't stop staring at the picture. The idea was irresistible. This was *exactly* what I wanted, and still do: to no longer be in danger, and to no longer be dangerous either. When I look at the picture now, I am struck dumb like the stone that Lot's wife was turned into.

Perhaps in our age of research and love of facts, it is not how to teach a myth we need to learn but how to listen. I don't want my students to suffer from a deficit of knowledge. I want them to know exactly where they came from—that long, slow splitting of lineages: Chordata begat Euchordata; Euchordata begat Craniota; Craniota begat Vertebrata. This is an easy fix. We don't remember the pain of our birth but feel every day the pain of our own impending death in the aging face of the one who gave birth to us. I would no more call belief in an eternity of petting lions and palm-feeding deer a disease than what Robinson Jeffers envisaged that day on the hillside, beneath the circling vulture, a vision that seemed to skip the first step in the stairway to heaven: having his orifices excavated. Imagination is both affliction and medicine: one when we think about our origin; the other when we think about our end. If my students ask *What happens when we die?*—enskyment, I would like to tell them. There is no such thing. But there should be.

TRESPASSERS

"Where should I look for the body?" my husband jokes, prodding me to tell him where I plan to go each time I leave for a hike on Wisconsin's Ice Age Trail, which follows the farthest reach of a glacier that retreated ten thousand years ago. I walk the trail like a child exploring lines on the face of a grandparent: here, joy; there, a long sadness. The glacier has left its impressions: winding ridges, sandy mounds, shallow depressions.

About 120 miles of this 1,200-mile national scenic trail, including the five or so miles I hike most often, lie on private land. I have always been a borrower of forests. I have never needed to own land but have always required neighboring one who does. For the first half of my life, in Maryland, I borrowed a forest of locust, sassafras, and red oak, fragmented by fields of hay and feed corn. The fields and forest, my parents said, belonged to "Wilhelm," the surname of a man I never saw, which dissipated like fog as I roamed his land. The fields led to a creek in a steep valley, easy to walk to, exhausting to walk from. My sisters and I made domed forts there from saplings, with crow's-foot carpet, little temporary households we could head in the absence of adults. When I go home for Thanksgiving, I traipse through this wood like a giant, showing up at a new neighbor's fence. He appears on the lawn. "I'm Nelson and Pat's daughter," I say. "I'm trying to get to the creek. Do you mind if I walk through your yard?" I quickly add: "I live in Wisconsin now," so he knows this won't be a daily trespass. He nods me on.

I have borrowed a forest of hemlock and beech split by a tannin-orange trout stream. The state of New Jersey properly lent this parkland to me. It was overpopulated with black bear, according to Homo sapiens. I boarded there in a Civilian Conservation Corp cabin that had become a graduate student dormitory at an environmental education center. In the crawl space beneath, in two successive seasons, lived a skunk and raccoon. One year, nearby in a fallen tree, two porcupines overwintered. When I tapped the tree with a broken branch, they moaned and grunted their presence. I met my husband in this forest. On its trails, I often carried a little half-him-half-me, but only in my mind, never in my body.

Currently, the fragment of forest I borrow—the Ice Age Trail's New Hope Segment—lies between County Trunk T and County Trunk Z in Portage County in central Wisconsin. It winds past numerous hidden kettle ponds, crosses through several invisible property lines, rolls up and down mounds of glacial till and even, at one point, channels through the hedge between two farm fields, a vein-like passage.

Soon, I hope, I will be hiking this borrowed trail with an adopted child, passing on whatever I can: where the yellow lady's slipper blooms and the spotted salamander performs his courtship dance. But what I borrow goes far beyond the forest I walk in or the child borne of other blood, to whom, in a particular way, I plan to bequeath my neighbor's land. I own nothing, even my own body a vast ecosystem from which I lease myself. Therefore, I may be able to make this child mine—as much as any child can belong to any parent—by creating the same wilderness around him, on him, and inside him that I have.

❃

Once, in the field behind that borrowed forest of locust, sassafras, and red oak, I found a goose with a golden egg. At least, that's what I thought I saw. Really, the goose was dead, and I beheld not an egg but an organ, a stomach or bladder, bloated, made of shiny inner skin that glistened in the outer world. What does it mean that—even if only for an instant— a fable was more believable than what I actually saw: the true architecture of the body?

It's hard to conceive of the body as anything other than whole. Recently, looking for salamanders, I circumnavigated every kettle pond along the New Hope Segment. The going was rough: a trail seems wonderfully wild until one leaves it and must break new ground with each footfall. Cutting across inclines, the foot shifts inside the shoe like a continental plate, causing blistery orogenies in surprising places—the inside of the big toe, the knuckle of the middle one. Your bushwhacking knees become tick magnets. I had just leapt over a narrow slough, sunk half my foot in mud. The water seeped into my left boot, ungluing the heel part. Then, there before me, lay the full skeletons of two bucks.

They lay close, as if they had curled together one cold winter night and not woken up. Bodies completely decayed, they lay like ancient aristocrats with their riches—two great racks: one six points, one eight—ready for the rut in heaven. I wanted the antlers. I gripped the end of one and gave it a tug, thinking the pedicel might snap from the skull like a floret of cauliflower, which it resembled. But what I felt instead was a strange kind of gravity, the pull of what this animal once was. The pedicel stayed fused to the skull. It was an anchor I could not heave up.

I remember when I first really comprehended that our bodies contain things—organs and interworking systems that keep us alive. On a favorite children's television show, I learned of Alexis St. Martin, a young voyageur who, in 1825, had survived a close-range gunshot wound to the abdomen. The program reenacted army surgeon William Beaumont observing digestion through the hole in St. Martin's stomach, which healed but never closed. In Beaumont's own words, the hole resembled a natural anus, minus the sphincter. I watched the actor playing Beaumont roughly push a finger into the hole and fish out a string he had placed there earlier, baited with pieces of meat and lettuce. I was horrified. It's difficult to believe in one's own entrails. We like to think we are indivisible, one important element, like iron, like gold.

Far from it. An adult human is a multicellular organism containing some thirty trillion cells, of two hundred different types. Our "wholeness" lasts but a few hours, when we are a single cell, just conceived, inside our mothers. Then we begin to divide. Within four days, our sixteen to thirty-two new cells, despite their identical DNA, differentiate and specialize into cells that will become our parts: a golden bladder, an acidy stomach, a leaden skeleton. One hypothesis for the evolution of multicellular organisms is that single-celled organisms of different species began to cooperate symbiotically, and over time their dependence led to a merger of their genomes into one organism. Perhaps this is why the idea of my liver, my lungs, my own heart—all the parts of me I can't see—feel so alien, so otherworldly.

But we are more complex even than that. The day I found the two buck skeletons, I had gone to the kettle ponds looking for salamanders. I know they like the water when they are mating and prefer the moist soil beneath the rocks and logs around the shore when they are not. From a salamander's perspective, the pond in its entirety is invisible, abstract, not a standalone thing. So, too, are our own bodies. In our mouths, in our intestines, even on our forearms live a host of microbes—good and bad—who are the center of their own universe. You are born into the world like a new continent, instigating great migrations from your mother's womb, her nipples, everything and everyone you touch. If the body's innards are hard to imagine, try to imagine its inhabitants: for every human cell your body contains, you also contain at least one resident cell of a bacteria, archaea, virus, or fungi.

Formerly, these facts merely intrigued me, but presently I savor them. Here's why: our biological parents give us twenty-three thousand genes, which have long been considered the building blocks of our identities; however, we also harbor eight million genes from the microbes we host, earning them the moniker "the second genome." As an adoptive mother, I won't be contributing any DNA to my future child, but maybe, just maybe, I can craft a bit of his microbiome.

"I contain multitudes," said Whitman in "Song of Myself," and he was right. The human body hosts 100 trillion microbes, which outnumber its human cells by approximately 1.3 to 1. Microbes constitute 2 to 6 pounds of the total body weight of a 200-pound adult, a number that shifts frequently from things like bowel movements or taking antibiotics. Much like the habitats of Earth, the biodiversity of the microbes on a particular area of your body is based on temperature and access to water. Your forearm, with just several dozen species living on it, compares to desert or tundra, not nearly as diverse as your warmer, wetter armpits, nostrils, ears, and inguinal creases (between your groin and legs). With hundreds to thousands of resident species, your gut is a veritable rainforest.

Not only did television first make clear to me that our bodies contain organs and inner-working systems, it also first revealed to me that healthy humans host all kinds of organisms. In the 1980s, my mother called me one night to look at the TV, some pop-news program like *20/20* on. The screen was filled with a close-up of human eyelashes, teeming with tiny creatures. "Ewww," she said, "look at these things that live all over us." The moment I looked at that *20/20* image, something new entered into me. I imagine it like the moment Columbus declared the earth round or Galileo proved the earth revolved around the sun. But such a shift— like Wegener's theory of continental drift, another paradigm changer—can take a long time to happen. I hold on to that moment, waiting for the day when conceptualizing myself as a singular being is as much nonsense as believing Earth is flat as a pancake.

Demodex folliculorum and *Demodex brevis,* or eyelash mites, inhabit the eyebrows and eyelashes and fine hair of the cheeks of about half the population, moving around our faces at night (they dislike light), using a retractable pin-like mouthpart to suck up dead skin cells and oil, spending their days facedown in our follicles like ostriches with their heads in the sand. They mate—fertilization is internal—lay eggs in a day and a half, which hatch in two days, reach maturity a workweek later, and die in two weeks—all on the surface of our faces. They are more commonly found on people age twenty or older, and are passed through physical contact, such as literally putting our heads together.

As far as we know, eyelash mites mostly don't influence us at all. Population booms may be connected with allergies in some individuals; in others, a bacteria that colonizes the eyelash mites' waste may be linked to a skin condition called rosacea, adding yet another layer to what makes us who we are: the things that colonize the things that colonize us.

I relish them all.

By far, the microbes we host affect us in positive ways—keep us alive, even—providing enzymes without which we wouldn't be able to digest food. They manufacture essential vitamins. They help us process the drugs we take and cleanse us of harmful chemicals. They promote cell restoration in the gut lining and trigger and assist our immune system. Journalist Michael Pollan writes that our individual microbiota exerts an influence on our health as great or possibly even greater than the genes we inherit from our parents.

The part I'm most interested in is how the microbes we host can affect complex choices we make, and what we consider our personalities. When you become a parent, you wonder what your child will grow up to be like, what he will get from you and other relatives, and how those things will combine to make him a unique individual. Chew on this: gut bacteria can drive the mating habits of flies; flies raised on starch preferred flies also raised on starch compared to flies who ate only molasses. Another study found that transplanting the gut microbes from easygoing, adventurous mice—whatever that means—into the guts of more anxious and timid mice made these mice more adventurous. Knowing that I can contribute to my child's microbiome gives me a power formerly held only by biological parents: the ability to shape his identity in a physical way. It pleases me that the experiences I give my adopted child may reside in more than his memory, that pieces of me may reside in more than his conscious being.

To learn more, I study Michael Pollan's article "Some of My Best Friends are Germs," my own *What to Expect When You're Expecting*. He explains that children raised in rural areas, who have greater contact with plants, animals, and soil, as well as those from cultures who raise their children communally, exposing them to many places and people, have more diverse bacteria. As on Earth, the more biodiverse your body's bacteria, the healthier you are likely to be. "The nuclear family," Pollan writes, "may not be conducive to the health of the microbiome."

It takes a village to raise a child. I will make mine healthy and happy, building on the microbiota picked up on his first ramble, through the canal of his birth mother's body. I will lay him in the soil, sit him in trees, dangle his chubby feet in the fecund pond, pile him over with leaves. I will lay down with him in the forest, hug him cheek-to-cheek, construct a little *Demodex folliculorum* bridge, bridges to everything. I will build his body in the way I can.

✳

One day, in my borrowed forest, I sat along the trail above a shallow pond set deeply in the land. Thoreau calls a lake the earth's eye, and that is how I saw it. I wished to observe not the workings of a pond but our planet's ocular system, how the earth sees. I wanted to extract, like Beaumont, strings of facts.

As I sat, something pushed a V across the surface. I moved from the rim down to the skeleton of an old beaver lodge, mudless and white, and zigzagged out over the water on the main beam, its branches, gnawed to points, both obstacles and handholds. I sat precariously, legs crossed so I touched the spine of the lodge at ankles and tailbone, the beveled edge of a branch poking my back, arched to keep my rear from aching. The original yoga, I mused.

My perch descended into the water six feet in front of me. On my left waited a cluster of wood-frog eggs in a cloud of algae and mud that could very well have rested on the back of a turtle. Suddenly, to my right, the V approached. I froze. A muskrat streamed over the log like a platelet or microphage moving through the pond's veins. I couldn't have placed him more squarely in the crosshairs of a telescope, magnified in the tannin-colored water made transparent by sun high in the sky.

Over the next few weeks, I continued to track the muskrat, finding his muddy mound of a home through the leafless trees in another pond I had largely ignored. I encountered his tail-dragging tracks near a low bridge, though morning, evening, and afternoon stakeouts by what seemed to be a feeding platform—a mat of mud and reeds in a cluster of cattails— did not reveal him. But while I waited for the muskrat, wood ducklings paddled through the algae-covered pond as they once did their own yolks. Irregular rows of scented pond-lily pads flapped like the ruffles of a summer dress in unseasonable winds, showing their red undersides. Blue flag buds, not yet open, pursed their petaled lips at my long intrusion. High up in a smooth stag completely shorn of bark, a family of pileated woodpeckers ducked angular red heads in and out, square pegs in a dark, round hole. Under three logs nestled clutches of tiny freshwater pearl-like eggs—either snail or salamander. One night, I hopscotched to the pond through a pleasant plague of micro toads. From a single spot, on successive evenings, I roused a small owl, twin fawns, and a gray tree frog; next to him under a downed branch hid a blue-spotted salamander. Since I had begun looking for one thing, I began to see everything else. I was looking for a muskrat, but I found a whole ecosystem.

Ecosystem: a term coined less than a century ago when the English botanist Arthur Tansley wrote: "[We] cannot separate [organisms] from their special environment, with which they form one physical system," a concept illustrated further by Wisconsin's own Aldo Leopold. When I worked as a naturalist in that borrowed forest of hemlock and beech, I would hike the children deep into the woods for a scavenger hunt and ask them to find, in addition to plants and animals, the environment's abiotic factors: water, minerals, sunlight. We are in the sun, actually: the heliosphere, the sun's outermost layer, extends beyond the orbit of Pluto, not hard to believe when you venture to the pond in the evening—working specifically around a muskrat's perceived schedule—and find you can see absolutely nothing due to the glare of the setting sun.

"The whole," Aristotle said in *Metaphysics*, "is something beside the parts." We can never be fully sentient of our design. We have a universe inside us—a system of interworking parts containing organisms with their own systems of interworking parts: all that pulsing, secreting, and dilating we're not conscious of. There are muskrats in our veins. When I seek out the muskrat, regardless of whether I spot his slick-furred foraging, if I see the pond he swims in, I see him. What we consider to be our selves may be a strange invention, a fragile construct between two truer things: the world we harbor and the world we anchor in.

Babies were once thought to be sterile inside the womb. Current research has begun to debate that point; scientists have found bacteria in the meconium, babies' first poop, which forms in utero. Likely, bacteria from the placenta breaks into the umbilical cord and begins populating inside the fetus's gut. But for sure, upon exit through the birth canal, your body is introduced to the bacteria living in your mother's vagina; then, as you are placed upon her, to bacteria from her skin; and finally, if you are breastfed, to bacteria from her nipples.

These first bacteria are important; the microbes you pick up in the birth canal help you to digest your first meal.

An analysis of one thousand fecal samples from the UK Adult Twin Registry, a group of twelve thousand volunteer twins, about half identical and half fraternal, indicates that the genome of the host affects what type of bacteria can inhabit it. In other words, your genome—those twenty-three thousand genes you inherit from your parents—to some degree dictate the types of bacteria that will, or can, take up residence on you. If, for example, you inherit genes that produce extra stomach acid, you will host slightly different gut bacteria than someone who inherits genes that produce less stomach acid.

This concerns me a bit. Am I just fooling myself? Without contributing to his genes, and without giving birth to my child, how will I get my bacteria into him?

I have been caught trespassing.

Even my husband scolds me, when I tell him about the path that I have made downhill from the Ice Age Trail by walking so much around the muskrat's pond, with which I have fallen in love. "That's private land," he warns, and then of the family who owns it, "If the Harts knew you were walking all over their property . . ."

"It doesn't matter. No one will see me. No one goes there," I say. The pond is deep in. It's not, as I may have implied, all bucolic. Around it resounds the constant high whine of mosquitoes like continuous semi-traffic on a distant road. Often, I have to undo my bun and comb my hair with my fingers in front of my face, like a wild child, to shield myself from the circling deerflies. Occasionally, one tangles in my locks and has to buzz its way out, alarming us both. There are periods in summer when I will only visit the pond on windy days, when the bugs can't find me. I pepper my hikes with sprints, trying to lose them like police on a chase.

Once, I got caught. Not at the muskrat's pond, but while I was walking the dog near our home, I stepped off the road to a marsh in somebody's woods, sat down on a tuft of grass, and let the dog off her leash to do her own exploring. I watched a group of ruby-crowned kinglets while a few cold wood frogs, which had silenced their chorus during my noisy arrival, resumed their quacking. The spring had been slow, and I wanted to see amphibians, to smell the thawed soil. Rather, I *needed* to.

My need may not have been quackery. Mice injected with *Mycobacterium vaccae,* a benign bacterium in the soil, produced more serotonin, a dearth of which is associated with depression in humans. When dropped into a bucket of water (who would do this?), these mice swam for twice as long before they began to passively float. They could also learn better: they ran mazes faster after merely inhaling the bacteria. Planting flowers, eating unwashed kale from your garden, sitting low in a neighbor's marsh, all of these can benefit the mind in ways similar to antidepressant drugs— yet another way in which microbes can influence our health and personalities.

But on that day, a truck drove slowly by, interrupting my psychotherapy. The driver's head turned exactly in my direction. I knew what was about to happen. I had seen the turkey hunters parked on the sides of the road and in the driveway of a trailer that was, for most of the year, vacant, and where, out front that day, someone had tied a little barking dog. I tried for a quick exit but was interrupted by a large bearded man with a black bow.

"This land's posted, ya know," he said.

"It's been such a cold spring," I tried to explain, but hung my head. What I wanted to say: I promise I won't take anything from your forest but the invisible medicine it provides.

*

It doesn't take long to find it: an article that gives a little proof that I can influence my adopted child's microbiome. Its title makes my heart flutter: "Nurture Trumps Nature in a Longitudinal Survey of Salivary Bacterial Communities in Twins from Early Adolescence to Early Adulthood." The study found no significant difference in composition of the oral microbiome between identical and fraternal twins, meaning our genetics has little or no role in the resident species of bacteria in our mouths (at least from ages twelve to twenty-four, the ages in this study). To me, it means a few thousand lip-kisses and shared popsicles, and my child will be of my body.

Although the bacteria of our biological mother are the first to colonize us, "Over time," according to the University of Utah webpage Your Changing Microbiome, "the early influence of the mother is diluted." Slowly, your microbiome will come to resemble your father's as much as your mother's, and then to other people you live with, biological relatives or not.

Everything you touch and interact with introduces you to microbes, including the skin bacteria of the doctors and nurses in the hospital, if you are born there, and the midwives, if you are born at home. Babies born through C-sections pick up different bacteria than babies born vaginally, and babies fed breast milk have different gut bacteria than babies fed formula. After age three, a person's microbiome becomes more stable and is similar to what it will look like through adulthood. It can shift in response to things like illness, disease, a course of antibiotics, stress, injury, pregnancy, and changes in diet, as well as developmental events like puberty and menopause.

Not a mother yet, I have no idea how easy it will be to share bacteria with my child: how crawling babies leave no surface—however dirty—unexplored; how many illnesses not only he but *I* will have those first two years; how intimate bodily functions become with a curious toddler; how many surfaces in the house, other than the toilet, will be soiled with poop and showered with pee; how much like farming those first two weeks of potty training will feel. "The world," says microbiologist Stanley Falkow, "is covered in a fine patina of feces."

I smile to think of my adopted child's toothbrush next to my husband's and mine, in its little holder on the bathroom sink just a few feet from our toilet, not out of reach of the spray from a flush. It's a spray as invisible as property lines, as invisible as borders from a peak I once climbed where I heard five states would be visible. I stood at the top of the mountain disoriented, overlooking a continuous lay of land unbisected by the dark borders on my map, in my mind. Maybe where we all come from is indistinguishable from where we all are now: maybe no line exists to mark where I end and you and the land begin.

One night I kneel by the water's edge just off my trail, again next to the muskrat's feeding platform. This is separate from his lodge, clear on the other side of the pond. I sit on a tiny rock—the only one available—surrounded by poison ivy. I sit for maybe an hour, willing the water-surface interruptions of whirligig beetles to turn into the work of a muskrat nose or tail. Then, all of a sudden, a single cattail falls like a tree, cut from its subaquatic base by some underwater lumberjack. I can almost hear the word *Timber!* It could easily have been severed by the jaws of a snapping turtle—I saw one on the shore looking for a nest site at almost this very spot a couple weeks ago—but I'd like to pretend it was the work of a muskrat.

There is much we cannot see, in the ecosystem and in ourselves. Perhaps when we look both outward and inward, we need to use only the coarse focus and increase our field of view, because what at first appears blurry may be actually the truest version of a thing. We are more than the amalgam of genes and memes we imagine ourselves to be; we have pigeonholed the soldiers in the nature-nurture squabble too narrowly, each more complex than we ever could have believed. We have been thinking of ourselves as persons, when we are more like the land. I see the pond; therefore, I see the muskrat. And the snapping turtle. And me. I wonder whose descendant will preserve my name—my husband's name really, mine long ago abandoned. I sit at the Hart's, or it could just as well be Wilhelm's. Forgive me my trespasses. I carry a surname lightly, just like the land.

BIG NIGHT

The US contains more species of salamander than any other country, but your whole life can pass without encountering one. Salamanders—secretive, fossorial, nocturnal—exit underground harbors only in darkness. Even those that gather in great masses to breed do so without a sound, moving monk-like through the yammering of wood frogs and spring peepers to ephemeral ponds.

In the country's eastern half, many folks would be surprised to find they share their neighborhoods with *Ambystoma maculatum,* the spotted salamander, a creature that looks like it belongs in the Amazon. Two uneven rows of big, bright yellow dots extend from head to tail on its dark, glossy body, a body I have always thought looks purple, though most field guides describe it as steel gray or black. Spotteds are stout and medium-sized; at four to seven inches long, they look like they'd make a good meal for something. But they're not easy to find. Scientists tracking them with radio telemetry, through tiny transmitters surgically implanted into the salamanders' midsections, discovered one spotted salamander living four feet underground. To find one of these brightly colored animals beneath a rock or within a log feels like hitting the jackpot.

My interest in salamanders renewed with surprising force the same spring my husband and I began the process of adopting a child. I had recently moved away from an area of high salamander density (from New Jersey, which has sixteen species, to Wisconsin, which has only seven) and ceased teaching environmental education; instead I was teaching English and spending my workdays indoors. Nevertheless, I aimed to be present for the annual nocturnal mass breeding of the spotted. There was a chance I would see them and a chance I wouldn't, these creatures that seem scarce but are relatively numerous, that live singly all year long but on a single evening gather in multitudes. My search for the spotted salamander contained the same odd combination of uncertainty and possibility that I needed to retain in my journey to becoming a parent.

What's more, the adoption process seemed at times rather cold-blooded. Mechanical. Deliberate. Too conscious. Take, for example, the initial paperwork, a long list of characteristics we had to decide whether we would accept in a child. We had checked "yes" for premature birth and low birth weight, and "maybe" for developmental delays and failure to thrive; "yes" for heart murmur, but "no" for heart defect; "yes" for cleft lip and club foot but "maybe" for epilepsy and microcephalus; "yes" for diabetes but "no" for hemophilia. Under both hearing and vision we'd checked "yes" for partial loss and "no" for total loss. Somewhat contradictorily, we'd checked only "maybe" for tobacco, alcohol, and drug use during pregnancy but "yes" for *no* prenatal care. We'd checked "yes" for criminal history in background, "yes" for mental illness, and "yes" for all the ethnic groups listed. We'd folded the paper into thirds, slid it into an envelope, and mailed it to the adoption agency we had selected, to enter it in the May lottery.

This was in March. As we waited to hear if we'd won, I needed something else to anticipate that, like a child, had as yet eluded me. I needed something to actively look for, something I couldn't be sure I would find.

Many have attributed the "child wish," as it is called rather poetically in scientific literature, to biology—an innate yearning necessary for survival. "This gazing at my child," essayist Lia Purpura writes, "is a kind of eating, it is that elementally nourishing." It seems reasonable to assume a species would die out if it did not have an inborn drive to create offspring. But natural selection would hardly hinge a species' survival to a desire for such a delayed effect. And for most of our evolution, we didn't even know what act created children. If the biological child wish were true, we would have been in peril—ingrained with a strong yearning for a particular end yet lacking any knowledge of how to achieve it, which would have caused extinction. By now the truth should be obvious: what we have an innate biological drive for is the *creating*, not the offspring. It's sex we want, not children.

It appears, though, as if the human desire for children is innate because it is so common; most people want to have children. According to the US Census Bureau's American Community Survey, in 2016, the number of women who had given birth ranged from 3 percent of teenagers aged 15 to 19, to 83 percent of women aged 45 to 50. So by the end of their childbearing years, most women have borne children—more than three-fourths, a solid majority. Of the 6.7 percent of married women, per the Centers for Disease Control, who have complete infertility, many seek alternative methods of fulfilling the child wish. In 2017, 1.7 percent of infants born were the result of assisted reproductive technology (ART), a number that does not include the likely high and rarely publicized number of failed ART attempts. In addition, .7 percent of all women ages 18 to 44, about half of whom already have a child through birth, have adopted.

These last two groups clearly want children. They've gone well beyond the mechanisms nature has provided to acquire them: the first may have induced ovulation with drugs and undergone multiple cycles of in vitro fertilization, accepted eggs into their bodies they did not create and sperm from men they've never met; the second has perhaps made uncomfortable decisions about the sort of child they want—its age, ability, race, and, for a little more dough, gender—and spent so much time preparing and signing paperwork, the process may begin to feel more akin to divorce than adoption. Both cases require significant amounts of money and entertainment of the child wish for much longer than the year it takes most people to have a child naturally. So—and I hesitate to ask this—when we go to such extremes to have a child, is it really the child wish we're fulfilling, or has the wish taken on some other nature? In other words, what exactly is it we desire when we desire children?

✳

I've always been fascinated by salamanders. Early on, I saw them retreating now and then beneath a ring of pioneer-laid stones around a favorite spring in the woods where I grew up. Later, walking off some adolescent woe, I leaned into a steep hill, brushed away leaves, and found the soil beneath so moist and rich with salamanders that I could hardly believe it. (Long before, there would have been unbelievably more:

the non-native earthworm, brought to America in European ship ballast, gobbles up the forest's leaf litter, leaving less to support our native invertebrates and, thus, fewer invertebrates to feed our woodland salamanders.) In my job as an environmental educator in New Jersey, I taught elementary and middle school students. Salamanders, if you knew where and when to look, were often the easiest thing to conjure up for a hundred city kids who had just two-and-a-half days to spend in the woods. Salamanders are more numerous than turtles. They are easier to catch than frogs. You kneel at a forest seep, fingers numb, lifting and replacing rocks wrapped in moss, one after another. Most reveal nothing. But then something happens in the mud lifted suddenly into the water from beneath an upturned stone: what looks like just the current of the stream escaping becomes a salamander.

In general, salamanders don't bite (though surprisingly, most do have tiny, flexible, cone-shaped teeth used for grasping prey). They don't pee on you like toads or musk you like stinkpots or mink frogs. They don't scare the hell out of you at first like snakes do. As long as you don't grab them by the tail (which would be cruel —many detach their tails in self-defense and leave them behind, wriggling wildly for the confused predator, then burn precious calories in tail regeneration), they are easy to handle. They seem relatively untroubled by capture, staring at you with dare-to-amuse me, Garfield-the-cat eyes. If you want to commune with an animal, salamanders can be an exquisite choice.

Many species, despite overall general population declines, are still shockingly numerous. "If you took all the salamanders in the forest and put them in a sack," I would say to my herpetology students at the environmental education center, "and then put all the small mammals in that same forest in a second sack, the sack of salamanders would be larger." Another comparison: salamanders make up more than 2.6

times the biomass of birds during the peak breeding season. Once or twice a year, my students didn't need these thought experiments; on a warm day after rain, there would be mass migrations of red efts, the toxic-looking—and, to a blue jay, toxic-tasting—juvenile, terrestrial stage of the eastern spotted newt. You couldn't walk without fear of crushing one. Those days were a great unplanned lesson on fulfillment and desire. With kids transporting efts by hand across roads and paths, adopting particularly cute ones as temporary pets, we never got where we were going. Where we were going became where we were. What we unearthed became what we had set out for.

Salamander courtship and breeding offer quite a few zoological surprises. Up to a third of red-backed salamanders are monogamous, a rarity for amphibians—though their monogamy, it turns out, is more social than reproductive. Many terrestrial salamanders guard their eggs, curling body or tail around their clutch in the kind of circumferential hug one might more reasonably expect of a canine or rodent. But perhaps nothing tops the reproductive behavior of the spotted, which, once a year, holds what can be described as none other than a bacchanalian nuptial dance that lasts into the wee hours of the morning.

No one is sure what drives the various species of *Ambystoma*, the mole salamanders, out of the networks of small mammal burrows they occupy singly for up to fifty-one weeks of the year, to mate in spring. Because they all appear at the same time, migrating to safe, fishless waters, herpetologists have come to call this event "Big Night." To *Ambystoma*, the essential factors for Big Night must be precise. But to us, with our calendars and thermometers and sling psychrometers, it's just another numbers game.

They emerge in the first warm rain after winter. How warm and how rainy is anybody's guess; different studies conclude different temperatures, and sometimes just fog or sudden snowmelt is enough. The most accurate predictor may have been right under our noses—or our feet—all along: in a ten-year study of mole salamanders in St. Louis County, Missouri, mass migrations started when soil temperatures a foot deep reached at least 40.1°F *and* the thermal profile reversed—meaning it was finally warmer at the surface than underneath.

On that aforementioned first warm, rainy night after winter, spotteds return to the place of their birth, likely aided by the smell of the water and plants of each particular pool. In experiments, blindfolded—yes, blindfolded—salamanders have easily been able to find their pools; intercepted adults preferred home pond odors to those of foreign ponds.

Then, under the water, the dance begins. According to James W. Petranka in *Salamanders of the United States and Canada*, the male contacts the female with his snout, once, twice, again, and again; she prods him in return each time. He circles her ceaselessly, rocking his head back and forth over her back and beneath her chin. Then, shuffling aside, he deposits several packets of sperm on substrate in the water, or on top of other males' deposits. Called spermatophores, these are six- to eight-millimeter tapering, gelatinous stalks with little calderas at the top holding the seminal fluid. The female searches for them, a sidestep with the back feet, a walk with the front. She chassés across the pond bottom, squatting over spermatophore after spermatophore, taking in seminal fluid with her cloacal lips. The mating usually occurs in groups of three to fifty or more, and with all that twisting and turning of spots, I imagine it must look like a sort of subaquatic Jackson Pollock painting.

Big Night can last from three days to over two months, but even when prolonged, breeding usually occurs in just a few major bouts. The point is not to miss it. Because I couldn't know when it was going to happen, by my logic, I needed to be at the water before it possibly could. So all through March I hiked to frozen pools. I wasn't wearing snowshoes anymore, but only because the trail was so packed, I didn't need them; if I stepped off the path, winter was still knee-deep.

Five years ago, after about four years of trying unsuccessfully to conceive, my husband and I gathered with several other couples at a local agency for an informational meeting on adoption. It was exactly the opposite of Big Night. There we were: the city's infertile, unfecund; no matter our achievements, unable to create in the most basic, most ancient of ways, in a way some people did by accident. There was no need to meet and greet. We knew all about each other—the baby-name books resignedly shelved amidst rows of travel guides, all the nonsensical things we'd considered, like postcoital headstands and egg-white lubricant. But in spite of the feel of defeat, the women's faces looked paradoxically triumphant—their determination to be mothers would not be trounced by this refusal of their unborn children to come into existence, to continuously pass out of them like tears, not solid but liquid. After receiving a fat folder of handouts, my husband and I paraded to our seats, navigating the circuitous route afforded by round tables butted up against walls in a small room. We sat down and took off our coats. I heard something but didn't move. Then, a voice:

"Your wallet," it said.

I turned and saw the source of the sound I had ignored. My wallet had fallen out of my pocket. It was now lying on the floor in the center of the room. The finger of the man who had watched it fall extended toward it, as if accusing us all of what it seemed we were about to do: buy something. Not a baby, of course. What was it we really wanted?

Although the child wish is not innate, it may still have natural underpinnings. Our biological clock is not set at "baby," but at more abstract things: security, love, esteem, meaningfulness. Such needs can be met in many ways, including having children. And the child wish, of course, like all human behavior, is heavily influenced by learning and environment. Perhaps no other period in history than the 1950s and 1960s, with its focus on the perfect family—think *Father Knows Best* and *Leave It to Beaver*—has made it seem as if not having children is abnormal, that if you choose to remain childless, you don't know what you are missing.

The child wish can be so strong, sometimes good people who want to be parents do desperate things. A week earlier, I had read a blurb in the US news section of my local paper about a man and woman who traded an exotic bird for two children. The guardian of the children originally wanted $2,000 for the boy and girl, four and five years old. But the couple, who had been trying unsuccessfully to get pregnant for years, did not have two grand, so they gave her $175 in cash and their $1,500 pet cockatoo.

The "adoptive" parents, according to the case detective, "had good intentions from what we see." But I had trouble believing this—that to buy a child, even to raise it as one's own, was not tainted with the same unlawfulness as to sell one. An economic transaction seemed no way to start a family. Weren't the buyers as much at fault as the sellers? After all, if there were no demand in the first place, there would be no supply. Isn't that how the law goes?

Dutch philosopher Paul van Tongeren has written that a paradox arises when "the manner in which we want something is in conflict with the nature of the thing we want." Although he seems to be writing primarily about the use of assisted reproductive technology, I can see how adoption also applies. According to van Tongeren, the child wish hinges on elements of surprise combined with unmatched love; we don't choose our children, and we love them unconditionally. What we desire when we desire children is actually a wild unbridling from choice and control—the most intense astonishment and rapture the universe can provide. Yvonne Denier, of Belgium's Center for Biomedical Ethics and Law, agrees: when we wish for a child, she notes, we want something that by its very nature escapes us, something we are unable to control attaining. We cannot decide to have a child, she writes, in the same way we might decide on a holiday destination, weighing pros and cons and choosing the characteristics we do and do not want.

Compared to the heat of passion in which one normally produces children, assisted reproductive technology and adoption can, at times, feel rather calculated. Beyond sex, fulfilling the child wish naturally is passive, a nine-month unraveling from womb to world governed only by imagination. It takes just two people. ART and adoption, in contrast, usually take much longer and involve crowds of stakeholders. Both feel deliberate, premeditated, a long road of things changing hands. ART can feel like playing God, disrupting natural selection, messing with the rhythm of the universe. We measure adoption's progress not by sonograms and tiny, knit caps, but in fits and starts of legalese and paperwork. At times, one worries that adopting means participating in a system that exploits the poor. One unhinges at the phrases "child laundering" and "human trafficking."

My husband and I left that day without filling out any paperwork, unable to pinpoint exactly what it was we wanted and reconcile that with how we were going to get it. We also never set foot in a fertility clinic. Five years passed. We met a couple who did not want to become parents, a friendship that did not require bracing ourselves for the inevitable phone call or dinner announcement that would change every second spent with them into a reminder of our inadequacies. We took up wine and mojitos and went to Paris. We got advanced degrees. Every month we buried the possibility of a child, until we had no more room for grief.

Once, teaching that herpetology session at the environmental education center, surrounded by fifth graders, I held a northern red salamander we'd just found. As I relayed some fact or another, the salamander began to writhe, opened its mouth, and out popped another, smaller salamander.

"It just had a baby!" one of the children shouted.

"No," I said after a moment, gently correcting him. "I think that was dinner."

Many salamanders, including the northern red, engage in cannibalism. The tiger salamander—the country's most widespread species—produces larvae that can develop to be either cannibalistic or not. When populations are dense, the cannibalistic morph appears. Through smell, it can tell whom it's related to and how closely they're related, preferring to prey on non-kin.

The fifth graders and I knew that amphibians don't have live births, and births don't originate from the same place as words. But what had happened seemed perfectly natural, expected even: something smaller had come from something larger. So I have to admit, looking down on what had occurred, feeling topsy-turvy from the moment, birth was also my first thought.

The tendency to see death as birth, or link the two in some way, is not all that unreasonable a leap. For an organism programmed for survival, recognition of mortality results in all kinds of tricks of the mind to reduce our anxiety, including, according to one study, increasing our desire for children. It makes sense: children offer both literal and symbolic immortality. They can carry on one's genes, one's beliefs, one's business, one's memory. Part of our wish for having a child is about reducing our fear of no longer existing.

Is this why, at age thirty-eight, sitting in an airport waiting for our plane after visiting my family at Christmas, watching worn-out parents trying to corral their spirited children, I turned to my husband, who had over the past five years often brought up adoption, and said, "Let's do it"?

Fear of death is hardly the only motivator for having children and certainly not a totally conscious one. There are a multiplicity of factors, measured by many tools: the "Reasons for Parenthood Scale," the "Parenthood Motivation Index," and, my favorite, mostly because of its title, which sounds like something a six-year-old might create to interview Santa Claus—"The Child Wish Questionnaire." I muddle through the research: a whole host of reasons for desiring children exists, ranging from happy early-childhood memories to the influence of organized religion and traditional gender roles to the belief that having a child around is "nice," makes one happy, and provides a unique relationship. Nothing is that surprising. What truly surprises is the reality of parenthood, which, most research suggests, decreases happiness. Much has been written about it. Roy F. Baumeister, in *Meanings of Life*, called this the "parenthood paradox." Perhaps the most-cited indicator of the lowered sense of well-being felt by parents is the fact that on one survey, women rated taking care of their children only slightly more positive than commuting and doing housework. This makes the great lengths that folks opting for ART or adoption go to even more curious.

＊

By April, the snow began to melt. I knew the time was approaching for Big Night. At work, vernal pools strung through my mind like the trail of shiny white pebbles laid by Hansel and Gretel. One night, I took the dog to the woods. In the past, she had stumbled upon a spotted salamander or two when we weren't even looking. But that night, when the beam from my headlamp, aimed at curious holes in the mud—probably openings where squirrels had buried and dug up nuts, or rained-out tracks from deer hooves—crossed before her, she just looked confused.

If even the dog was flummoxed, I thought, how would a baby feel? We had received a return letter from the adoption agency confirming our entry in the May lottery, but with no information regarding when or where it would happen, or how they would deliver the results. I worried. *Could a baby do this?* I wondered.

Could you bring a baby to the woods on a rainy, cold night? Sit it on your hat or gloves laid side by side—like you sometimes do yourself—on top of the wet grass, while you moseyed around looking for amphibians? A fear overtook me. How would I change as a parent? Would I leave my baby at home with my husband while I went on amphibian hunts? Would I stop hunting altogether? I didn't find any salamanders that night, but when I got home and took off my clothes to shower, I did find the first tick of the season. Ticks don't faze me. But how would I feel if I found this tick crawling over the pudgy little kneecap of my amphibian-hunt-spectating baby?

A certain level of ambivalence toward parenthood is common. A 1997 study in the *Journal of Marriage and the Family* found ambivalence toward childbearing in 20 percent of young couples. A 2010 *Journal of Reproductive and Infant Psychology* article concludes that ambivalence toward childbearing is "widespread." And the 2012 National Center for Health Statistics reports that 37 percent of US births are unintended, meaning mistimed or unwanted—more than a third. Particularly for women, to whom most childbearing and rearing responsibilities still fall, and who may likely anticipate all these responsibilities before birth more accurately, whether or not to have a child is a complex issue.

What's more, the intense social pressure to have children may have originated relatively recently. For much of human history, having a child was dangerous for women, carrying with it a high risk of death. In Western Europe, for centuries, a quarter of women remained childless. Though this was not likely by choice but due to poverty, political turmoil, or men away at war, the point is that the relative pressure on women to have children in order to feel "normal" has not been a constant in human history.

Statistics show the culture is again changing. One study followed 12,700 UK women born between 1950 and 1960 through their mid-forties. Seventeen percent are childless. That number was 10 percent for those born in 1946 and rose to 19 percent for those born in 1960. Delaying parenthood has birthrates down in multiple countries: Greece, Switzerland, Britain, Japan, Canada. While delaying parenthood doesn't necessarily mean couples will remain childless, it does alter the idea that childlessness is selfish, shameful, or to be pitied.

A married friend of mine who decidedly does not want children—never has, never will—once asked her mother, who had another girl and two boys (all healthy, all successful), what she thought about having children. The reply: "If I could do it again, I wouldn't." My friend was pleased with the answer, which vindicated her own feelings. And yet, of course, she would not exist if this woman had not conceived her.

Chances of becoming pregnant through one cycle of ART—which costs $12,000 on average in the US, an amount rarely covered by health insurance—are 40 percent for women aged 35 and under, 30 percent for women aged 35–37, 22 percent for women aged 38–40, 13 percent for women 41–42, and 6 percent for women older than 42. Despite less than promising odds for even the youngest age bracket, each year, more than 85,000 women choose ART, on average requiring three cycles (over $36,000) to have a "live birth," a clinical-sounding term which includes any baby born alive, even those who won't survive.

Adoption may seem like less of a gamble: if you have unlimited funds, inconceivable patience, and openness to a child with any type of needs, you will end up a parent. But most people do have boundaries. When I looked at the numbers, I was comfortable with the $3,000 required for a home study and initial fees, even though I knew we might never be chosen by an expectant couple considering adoption. But I worried about the unpredictable amount we might pay for prenatal care, legal fees, and counseling to an expectant mother who could understandably change her mind at some point during the pregnancy or (in Wisconsin) the thirty-day period after birth (called a "false start"—for the majority, 72 percent of false starts cost less than $5,000); the possibility of this happening multiple times (38 percent of adoptive parents have at least one false start); or, in the unlikely chance a birth mother with whom we were matched gave birth to a baby with serious defects (chances: less than 4 percent), that we would make the decision to walk away. If we did, our losses would be big: the entire cost of the adoption (usually around $25,000), any hope of ever becoming parents, and our own integrity.

I wondered how we would fund an adoption should we win the agency's ironically dubbed lottery. I did some research; one article listed loans, hard-to-get grants, and ideas for saving up this large chunk of money, ending rather ridiculously with the idea of garage sales and bake sales. *Leave no stone unturned,* the last line said.

ART and adoption both involve uncertainty, though hardly the type von Tongeren and Denier describe that characterizes the child wish. Any uncertainty involved in ART and adoption clashes with a cavalcade of consciously and carefully considered decisions, procedures, phone calls, and appointments. Often, you must move forward deliberately in the face of crushing defeat. The child wish can become a child obsession. Why do people do it?

I found more insight on the answer to this question not from studies of parent motivation among couples considering IVF or adoption (such studies tend to give results not that different from studies of those trying to conceive naturally), but in studies of problem gambling. Research on gambling addiction illuminates how we make decisions, how we respond to personal gains and losses, and why we take risks. Humans seem to be drawn to the astounding occurrence, regardless of its likelihood of happening. We are traditionally bad odds makers. We believe a win is likely after a series of losses, just as we expect sun after a week of rain, or, if looking for salamanders, vice versa—though here our assumptions may be correct, as weather does follow patterns. We abhor cognitive regret—stopping something too early and missing out on the next big reward—and are driven by a drive to recoup our losses. There is always the possibility that, although we never know where or when we'll hit it, a big win is just around the corner. *One more rock overturned,* one of my sources said, *and you'll find dinner.*

At times, the closer it got to the adoption lottery, I was no more distressed about losing than I was about winning. I began, salamander-style, to get cold feet.

The adoption lottery seemed a bit unconventional, despite being hosted by a licensed Christian social service organization of Wisconsin and Upper Michigan. When my husband and I first heard of it, I imagined that if they drew your application, somewhere instantaneously, a stork that would soon appear above the thatched roof of your house was plucking a baby from the pond where all little children lie—according to the Hans Christian Andersen tale—"dreaming more sweetly than they will ever dream in the time to come." It seemed almost too good to be true.

The prize, though, if they drew your application, wouldn't be a baby but acceptance into the agency's domestic infant program, just the start of the sometimes multiple-year process of becoming an adoptive parent. It's a popular agency, probably because of its long, successful history of providing good counsel to birth parents and adoptive families, as well as its reasonable fees. So, instead of dealing with a never-ending wait list, they hold a biannual lottery.

At the meeting required to enter the lottery, we were told that on two unspecified dates—one in early May and one in early November—social workers from the organization's various offices throughout the state would gather together, number the applications, put the numbers in a hat, and blindly draw a predetermined quantity. After we mailed in our application, I wondered often about this event. I imagined tiny slips of paper—the one with my number on it, for instance—blowing off a table when someone exited or entered the room, leaving me with no chance at all of being picked. Was there a lottery witness? Did a senior citizen stand against the wall, hands joined together solemnly as on so many states' televised daily lotto picks, to ensure everything went fairly and squarely? And if, as the social worker informed us, we would be allowed to reconsider the items we marked on the application at a later date—whether we could parent a child with microcephaly or one whose mother had a serious mental-health diagnosis, for instance—why was it even on the lottery application in the first place? Was this really some kind of weeding-out process? I imagined the social workers—all women, most likely mothers themselves—laughing wildly at those whose applications indicated a desire for the perfect child, ripping them up, and trashing them immediately. If this truly was a lottery, why not just have us write our name and number on the back of a raffle ticket and, if our ticket were drawn, consider the hard questions later?

Some psychologists believe gambling mirrors sexual excitement, with its buildup, climax, and release of tension over and over. Maybe this is why the idea of the adoption lottery excited my husband and me so much, why we chose this agency over others where we could have signed a contract and jumped right in to the adoption process. It felt natural to begin parenthood this way: to cast our lot, and then wait a month or two to see what happened.

✳

Mid-April rolled around. I still had not seen a single salamander. One weekend, the forecast was warm and rainy, but
I was busy entertaining a friend who had flown in to visit.
On Saturday she slept in, and I grabbed an umbrella to walk
the dog and check out an overflow area near our lake, finding
two deep open, holes: turtle hatchlings must have overwintered in the nest and emerged in the last few days. It was a
sign of something—but as of yet, I saw no amphibians.

We hung out all weekend. On Sunday morning, we
missed a call from my husband's little brother. On Sunday
night, it was still raining. He called again, and my husband
disappeared to talk to him. He returned to announce that his
brother's wife was pregnant—twelve weeks pregnant, with
identical twins.

I left my husband and guest to hunt for salamanders.
Many factors were at work, and I don't deny any of them. The
major mistake in psychology may be the belief that awareness changes behavior. It doesn't: we like our social pressure,
our sorrow, our envy. I knew I should be overjoyed by the
prospect of two new nieces or nephews—and I was—but I
admit I was also irritated, as if there were some kind of cos-
mological math occurring that didn't add up: two babies for
them, and zero for us.

I drove the streets past every pond I knew, looking for
slick salamander bodies in my headlights, wondering how
many I was running over in my desperate quest. But it began
to snow. In the morning, five inches would cover the ground.
I became dizzy from the winding country roads, staring into
the oncoming flakes with my brights on. The seasons ran
through my mind, lapping one another. They tangled in my
brain, and I couldn't shake the feeling that I'd missed some-

thing. Even though I knew it was still too early, it felt too late.

＊

A week or so later, I bought a pair of boots—no matter that I should be saving money—at the local Fleet Farm, the kind kids wear to jump in puddles. (Obstetricians wear them too, I recently found out from a friend, whose son's birth proved messy and more difficult than the norm.) I couldn't believe I was still traipsing around the shores of ponds all these years without them. I also couldn't believe I was still traipsing around the shores of ponds at my age, a kitchen strainer in hand. I knew I should be shuttling kids to soccer practice, piano lessons, laundering the clothes of pond-traipsing *kids*. Was there something wrong with me? Because I didn't have children, I couldn't stop being one? I felt like a ten-year-old boy, not a thirty-eight-year-old woman. In an old army ammunition plant near Madison, Wisconsin, a reservoir contains a population of tiger salamanders that, in adapting to their enclosed environment, have become neotenic, retaining for life their juvenile characteristics—feathery gills, keeled tails. They still reproduce, but along with their children, they never leave the water to live on land, as do most adult tiger salamanders. Officials want to drain the reservoir, regarded as a safety hazard, but locals are working hard to preserve it and its salamander population.

The day before Easter, I hiked to a pond a couple miles into the forest. It was dry and warm, so still I didn't find any salamanders. I was reluctant to put on my boots, which I had been carrying in a backpack. Finally, as I didn't want to have carried them in vain, I slipped them on and waded into the water. That is when I saw them.

All over the substrate, on submerged sticks and grasses, like a thousand tiny glass slippers, lay the spermatophores of now-vanished male spotted salamanders. I picked up a stick where a salamander had laid three in a row to examine them more closely. They were translucent, the size of half your pinky fingertip. You might think they were some kind of tree mold or something a snail left behind. They littered the bottom of the pond like confetti, evidence of the start of the salamander new year. Upon further inspection, I found floating beneath last year's submerged cattail leaves loose constellations of eggs coalescing into infant galaxies.

I wanted to pick them up, but two feet was as far as I could go. I began to sink a little, and water threatened to deluge my boots. I was in the muck.

Despite knowing that the day-to-day tasks of raising an infant (changing diapers, doing laundry, cleaning up vomit) and raising a teenager (worrying, feeling hated) are unlikely to increase my happiness, and that social pressures to have children and labels of selfishness for the childfree are diminishing, I have not lost my child wish. Perhaps my (and others') child wish is so strong because the paradox of parenthood was nonexistent in the ancestral evolutionary environment. When we lived in small clans and tribes, children weren't such a drain on just two people. The "village" helped to care for the howling, nocturnal infant, and adolescence wasn't an issue because children began their own families at puberty.

So say Sonja Lyubomirsky and Julia K. Boehm of the University of California, Riverside, in their 2010 article, "Human Motives, Happiness, and the Puzzle of Parenthood." Furthermore, they point out that studies indicating a correlation between parenthood and decreased well-being have a severe limitation: it may not be possible to measure the kind of joy we receive from hanging out with kids.

Consider this: when my nephew was a baby (he is twenty-three now), I carried him along on a hike with my mother and his two sisters. We jumped over puddles in ATV trails where, annually, American toads laid their jellied egg strings and descended to the creek where my father had often taken my sisters and me as children. A soft wind blew aspen leaves from the trees. I took in the whole scene. But then my attention was caught by something I will never forget: my nephew's long moment of focus on a single leaf falling to the creek, from sky to water's surface. It was the first he had seen the likes of this. He had no room in his head for the big picture, for cycles and seasons and laws of physics. His life thus far was a patchwork of private astonishments. Maybe this is what children give us.

The night of Easter was warm and humid. When I walked the dog, the spring peepers were deafening, like some kind of unoiled mechanism inside my ears. Despite my previous day's discovery of the eggs and spermatophores, I reasoned that maybe a bout of latecomer breeding would happen again that night.

Back home, sweating, I sat in a chair facing my husband, who was on the couch typing up his doctoral thesis.

"I feel like tonight is the night." I said. "It's foggy. It's still sixty degrees. And it's very humid."

I was surprised when he put his laptop to the side and grabbed his camera to accompany me. We made the brief drive to the pool. Right away, when we exited the car, I saw something dark and glossy in the middle of the road. A salamander. Not the spotted but the blue-spotted: slightly smaller and more slender, deep indigo on top, cloud-colored on the bottom, with sky-blue speckles. Blue-spotteds also migrate to vernal pools in great masses, though their mating dance is more private as they pair off in the water, spread out, and lay their eggs mostly singly, attached to underwater vegetation.

When we entered the woods, we were in new territory. My husband and I have spent plenty of time outside in daylight hours, and certainly done our share of camping, but this was the first time we'd been out and about in a dark wood. It was unexpectedly pleasant. Something rustled, a sound that when we shined our lights at the ground we were surprised to find came from leaves lifting over worms pushing out of the soil. For a while we saw nothing, but when we got closer to the water, they started appearing, every five feet or so: a blue-spotted salamander, same as the one we saw on the road.

"This is a good pool," my husband declared, and I felt a small surge of affirmation. "I wonder if there are any in the frog pond by my work."

"The frog pond?" I asked, curious.

"The overflow area by the lake."

We went to check it out, along with another pond nearby. The night was perfect. We labored for hours, covering ground we'd never walked in daylight. Even though we saw no nuptial dancing, it was clearly a Big Night for blue-spotted salamanders. I'd never seen so many. We didn't get home till after midnight and fell into bed, exhausted.

We did not win the lottery. The news was delivered in the mail along with another child characteristics checklist— blank, to be pondered all over again—and an invitation to enter the next lottery, which would occur in November. Earlier, we had also received a large manila envelope enclosing a poster-sized drawing of "Quinn County." My niece, for a school assignment on mapping, had named a district after us. I wondered what part of that child's mind, who lives eight hundred miles away and whom I hadn't seen for a few months, I occupy. What word ignited her memory of me, brought me into existence in a place I no longer inhabit, to be gifted with a whole province?

We must never balk at unfamiliar territory. The worlds we discover, like those unanticipated red eft migrations that so engrossed my students or the midnight parade of blue-spotted salamanders my husband and I encountered, are often more astounding than what we set out for. The truth is this: no one is desperate for a child until they can't have one. The child wish is an art. We may entertain it any way we want as long as we know it is not about fulfillment. We must recognize that the laws mothers lay across the land—the grass is always greener, life is a gamble—were writ by the universe long ago, and to live fully, we must embrace them.

Finished with lotteries, I picked up the phone and called another adoption agency that had openings. I would, I decided, burrow beneath the bills and contracts, let them occupy a level I was not fully conscious of, as do those fossorial creatures I so admire, surfacing and resurfacing for the false starts. I would invite the ambivalence and uncertainty that accompanied my original wish for a child, which is what, finally, defines it. Right then all I felt was calm. It was a calm that allowed me to imagine what it would look like, if I ever found those spotted salamanders on Big Night, in the beam of my flashlight: the yellow spots on their backs a hundred gold coins tossed into a fountain—the child wish, in whatever way it would, unraveling.

BEGETTING

Spring was done. Wood frogs, peepers, spotted and blue-spotted salamanders—all explosive, early communal breeders—had fanned back out from the wetlands to their three-season forest haunts; tadpoles and salamander larvae had wriggled from clusters of eggs, infiltrating the surrounding water like post-big-bang particles in expanding space; and now the pond simmered beneath lily pads, algae, and duckweed that mostly concealed these aquatic young. Instead of lifting the pond's lid, I turned to the forest, hoping to unearth the eggs of the later-breeding red-backed salamander, *Plethodon cinereus,* a common terrestrial salamander with an uncommon habit: eggs laid on land, a larval stage completed entirely inside the egg—blasphemy for an amphibian.

Despite not leading the "double life" that characterizes amphibians (the Greek *amphi* means both, *bios* means life) by spending its youth on land, the female red-backed salamander still must keep her eggs moist. To do this, she curls her body around the eggs in some damp microhabitat on the forest floor. I found such a microhabitat uphill from the pond

beneath a particularly rotten, moss-covered log that prom-
ised to stay moist through summer. Sure enough, beneath it
lay a cluster of tiny, pearl-like eggs, and half a foot away, the
slender, tapered body of a red-backed salamander.

Naturally, I assumed the eggs were hers.

I know—*cum hoc, ergo propter hoc*: with this, therefore
because of this. Or the slightly more popular *post hoc, ergo
propter hoc*: after this, therefore because of this. In other
words, false cause. Commit it to memory now: *correlation
does not imply causation*. This logical fallacy had us believing
for centuries in spontaneous generation—that living things
could spring from the nonliving. Rotten meat spawned flies.
Moldy grain generated mice. Mud from the flooded Nile
bred frogs. Because the animals suddenly appeared in those
environments, the environments themselves, our forbearers
deduced, must have caused them.

"Correlation does not imply causation!" I drill into the
heads of my students at the community college where I teach.
We listen for the fallacy in news reports and campaign ads,
triumphant whistle-blowers. My students will not be fooled,
I think smugly. Yet I have been.

The first time I discovered a vernal pool full of amphibian egg clusters, the air rang with the earsplitting chorus of
the spring peeper, a type of tiny tree frog. The eggs must be
theirs, I thought. I didn't realize my mistake until more than
two years later when, hiking with a friend, we came across
that same combination. I shared my earlier experience, which
I mistook for knowledge. "I believe you," he said, holding
an adult-sized, less than one-inch-long spring peeper while
pointing to an egg mass in the water easily three-and-a-half
inches in diameter. "I'm just having trouble understanding
how *that* came out of *this*."

It did seem odd, so I went home to research it. Although
the female spring peeper can lay up to 1,200 eggs in a breed-

ing period, she lays her eggs singly, not in masses, and each egg is about the size of the period at the end of this sentence. The eggs we had found, that I had been finding for years, were laid by a creature which, at that point, I did not even know existed: the elusive spotted salamander, which lives underground, emerges to breed in essentially one night, then disappears. My mistake wasn't as silly as believing life could spring from the nonliving, but still I was ashamed. How many had I misled?

Cum hoc, ergo propter hoc is a pretty ho-hum human cognitive error. It happens all the time. A common example is the belief that cold, wet weather causes sickness. People do get sick more in winter than in summer, and the unpleasant change in weather seems the culprit. But like that elusive spotted salamander, there lurks in many of our basic assumptions about the world a third, confounding variable, the true cause of some effect: in this case, viruses and bacteria. Some pretty odd experiments have been designed to prove that microbes, not bad weather, cause illness. In one, research subjects either wore coats in a freezer, wore only underwear in a sixty-degree room, or wore wet socks and swimsuits while walking around hospital hallways. Then, doctors dripped infected mucus into their noses, along with a control group not exposed to wet or cold. There was no significant difference in the number of colds developed by any of the groups. Although more recent research does indicate that cold weather's effect on cells in the lining of the nose may lower the immune system's ability to fight off viruses and bacteria, the correlation between winter and illness seems to be more social than anything: cold weather means people stay indoors in close contact, passing along infections. Yet all winter long at work, I hear students and colleagues alike complain that the nasty weather is making them sick. In a more detrimental example, at the same time that US vaccination rates rose, so did diagnoses of autism, a correlation that caused wary parents to jump to the conclusion that vaccinations caused the disease.

In a study on public understanding of correlation versus causation, researchers at the University of Wisconsin-Eau Claire found that people inferred causation from noncausal data as often as they did from causal data, and that their causal inferences were influenced by their common-sense beliefs about a topic. In other words, the general public doesn't understand experimental design very well and tends to hear, or read, what they already believe. Humans are, as the authors put it, "cognitive misers" who rely too heavily on sometimes-correct but far-from-perfect built-in thinking biases, such as the tendency to see patterns. If event B happened immediately after event A, and the two events seem related, A must have caused B.

My own cognitive errors regarding correlation and causation have hardly been harmful: two years confusing a spotted salamander egg cluster with the ovum of the spring peeper caused nothing more than passing embarrassment. But I have other eggs to be concerned about now. Somewhere, inside some other woman, is the egg of a child I have set out to adopt. As I indicate on my adoption profile whether I am willing to accept a birth mother who smokes or uses drugs or has a history of anxiety or depression, I am anxious about what these factors of the genetic and prenatal environment might cause in my future child. As a soon-to-be parent, I must know what begets what.

Every couple of days, I checked the progress of the supposed red-backed salamander eggs. The log, moist as it was, fell apart in my hands, gradually increasing in pieces like a puzzle whose difficulty magnified each time I put it together. Where did the knot belong? Carefully, several times a week, I took apart and reassembled the log, drawing up leaf litter around it, shaking slugs from my hands, worrying about drafty new cracks that might dry out the moist micro-habitat. The red-backed salamander never revealed herself again. But her eggs multiplied, from one cluster to two, to three, to four, to five, as if—impossibly—eggs were begetting eggs.

Occasionally the eggs in a cluster would desiccate into tiny, deflated beach balls, but if this was hatching, I never saw any young. I had told my husband and a few friends that I had found the landlocked eggs of *Plethodon cinereus,* but I was beginning to have misgivings. At home, I checked field guides and googled images of red-backed salamander eggs, made notes about diameters and clutch sizes. At about two millimeters in diameter in groups of often more than ten, what I was looking at were too small and too numerous, I finally decided, to be the eggs of the red-backed salamander. They were simple snail eggs. I'd done it again.

Assuming causation where only correlation exists is the news media's most common error when reporting on scientific studies, according to George Mason University's nonprofit and nonpartisan Statistical Assessment Service. Jon Mueller, professor of psychology at North Central College in Illinois, compiled an intriguing list of headlines from public press articles for his students to scrutinize for evidence of the cor-relation/causation fallacy: "Fear of Hell Makes Us Richer," "Smiling Increases Longevity," "Eating Pizza Cuts Cancer Risk," and "Higher Beer Prices Cut Gonorrhea Rates." The pattern seems to be this: the headlines imply causation, while the article, generally somewhere in the middle, describes a study that indicates only correlation. Usually, quotes from interviews with the study's authors or from the actual text of the study reveal the lack of causation. It's all in the verb choice. In the headlines above, *make, increase,* and *cut* each imply causation. But none of the studies controlled for that lurking third variable. For example, the first study involved only a simple comparison between the per capita incomes of thirty-five countries and their citizens' self-reported belief in hell. While certainly the correlation is of interest (the higher the percentage of the population that believes in hell, the higher the per capita income), there are a host of other economic, social, cultural, geographic, historical, and political factors that contribute to a country's standard of living.

In order to show causation, a study needs to be experimental. Think back to fourth-grade science. A sound experiment contains a control group and a group exactly the same with the exception of one variable. When both groups are subjected to the same situation, any differing effects can be attributed to that variable, proving, in essence, that one thing has caused another. Properly designed experiments can reveal some surprising causes and effects. For example, "Washing Hands Reduces Moral Taint" (a link on Mueller's website), seems sensationalist. How could one prove such a thing? But the article reveals three fascinating studies of sound experimental design. In the first, subjects who had just recalled unethical deeds produced more cleansing words when given word fragments to complete than subjects who had not just been prompted to recall unethical deeds. In the second, subjects who hand-copied an unethical story then rated several products such as soap and toothpaste higher than subjects who had just copied an ethical story. And in the third, subjects who had just recalled an unethical deed from their past and were then offered a sanitary wipe upon exit were less likely to help a desperate graduate student than those who had recalled the unethical deed but had not been offered a sanitary wipe. In each of these, the researcher has manipulated one variable in a random sample of the population, proving that washing hands does indeed cause people to feel relief from some moral stain (at least, for *this* sample in *these* situations—it is difficult in social research to ascertain that results are generalizable to the entire population and transferable to other situations).

Proper headlines for studies that show only correlation read like this: "Migraine often Associated with Psychiatric Disorders," "Teen Drug Use Linked to Truancy," "Breast-fed Children Found Smarter." In these cases, *associated, linked,* and *found* imply only that the two events or conditions have occurred together. Modifiers like "often" or "tend" further indicate that only a correlation exists. Correlational studies are common and important because they offer directions for further research. But before more research occurs, it's impossible to know whether a causal link exists, or, if it does, the direction of causality. For instance, does teen drug use cause truancy, or does truancy cause teen drug use? Do migraines lead to psychiatric disorders, or do psychiatric disorders lead to migraines? Here, both researcher and journalist seem aware that correlation does not indicate causation. I, too, know this. Yet when I read these headlines, regardless of the researchers' and journalists' careful use of language, I can feel my brain, wholly on its own, take that extra step: *because I won't be able to breastfeed, will my adopted child struggle in school?*

My students and I puzzle over the diction in a few headlines on Mueller's webpage. "Dogs Walked by Men are More Aggressive." "Disciplinarian Parents Have Fat Kids." *Are* and *have* simply imply an observation has been made, we say at first. But moments later, each headline feels more like a decree. This *does* happen, and therefore, *will* happen, the headlines seem to be saying. *Watch out.* Our understanding flips back and forth, like changing lenses on a microscope.

With this, therefore because of this. Where would we be without it? It's one of the founding ways we make sense about the world around us. When the clouds darken, it rains; when it rains, plants grow. Therefore, therefore . . . But too soon we must learn to cultivate vigilance against our own perceptions, as if our brains evolved to interpret a simpler life on a more orderly planet; all of us, without a clear understanding of the scientific method, intellectually barren.

One day, on the hunt for red-backed salamander eggs, a full family of pileated woodpeckers, clinging low to several trees and therefore at eye level as I trekked up the hill by the pond, pulled me in a different direction. I tried turning over a log larger than the logs I normally selected. It split in my hands, an important lesson, because for weeks I had simply been looking under things rather than within them. This log revealed not what lay beneath but what it held: a cornucopia of amphibians. Like an illustration from a children's book, the neck and tail and two of the legs of a blue-spotted salamander peeked out of one cavity; out of another extended the back half of a central spotted newt. And there, attached to a middle cavity by a mucousy pedicel rested a clutch of red-backed salamander eggs. Twice the size of the ones that had been fooling me, each egg measured four millimeters instead of two. The clutch contained only eight eggs total. The female's midsection and tail curled around the entire clutch, just as the field guides indicated. This time, what I had found was unmistakable. I lay down, head in the soil, to snap a few pictures with my cell phone and was startled when a larva, like the pupil of an eye, turned inside its cloudy orb, as if checking me out too.

＊

At age ten or eleven, I aimed to read the entire Bible, six verses a night. Just a few chapters into Genesis, I found exhaustively long lineages interspersed with the familiar stories: *and Irad begat Mehujael: and Mehujael begat Methusael: and Methusael begat Lamech.* I wanted to read every word, so I pressed on: *and Mizraim begat Ludim, and Anamim, and Lehabim, and Naphtuhim, and Pathrusim, and Casluhim (out of whom came Philistim) and Caphtorim.* Sometimes, propped up in bed with the King James version of the Holy Bible in my lap, I endured weeks upon weeks of begetting.

Over a decade later, I was asked by a kindly professor what I wanted to do with my life.

"Have a child and raise it," I said. But it would be thirteen years, and I would be thirty-nine, before my husband and I, infertile, would adopt a child.

As part of the adoption process, adoption agencies ask prospective adoptive parents to indicate what kind of child they would like to parent, usually by checking yes, no, or maybe on a long list of characteristics. The list begins with things likely to have already been considered, such as age, race, and a general category of special needs. What follows becomes much more detailed than one could, or would like to, imagine, with all kinds of levels of disability—deaf, blind, club foot, cleft palate; and situations—such as a child who is the result of rape or incest, or whose birth parents have a criminal history or mental illness. Mental illness, but not criminal history, is broken down even further, despite the fact that extremely violent behavior, defined as committing ten or more homicides, attempted homicides, or batteries, has been linked to two genes—MAOA and CDH13. (No such link has been found for nonviolent crimes such as drug or property crimes.) Regardless, under mental illness you can choose anxiety, depression, schizophrenia, or *any*, a choice that brings on the same consternation as when *all of the above* suddenly pops up on a multiple-choice test. Then onto pre-natal care: smoking, alcohol and drug abuse are options, and this time you can also select *none*, which may be more like *all of the above*. The list of items to check (or not) can feel so horrifying as to make you want to stop the adoption process altogether, until you remember your own alcoholic, verbally abusive grandfather on your mother's side as well as that story you heard (only once) about your great-aunt finding your father's mother standing over your infant father, in his crib, with a knife. That gives you a little perspective.

So, too, does considering your own imperfections. Four years into marriage when I casually mentioned to my doc-tor that I had stopped taking the birth control pill because I would one day like to have a family, she urged me to take a multivitamin every day for the folic acid, proven defini-tively to reduce birth defects. (She did not mention their correlation when taken in late pregnancy, according to one study, with an increased risk of childhood asthma at three-and-a-half years as well as persistent asthma.) Nonetheless, I couldn't do it. The pills were too huge—horse pills—and I just couldn't start every day gagging. "If you're not using birth control," my doctor had said, "you *will* get pregnant," which, I guess, is the truth for most people. Over the years, that statement gained more and more irony. Yet still, through a decade of infertility, I was never able to sustain taking a mul-tivitamin for more than a few days at a time. Vitamins don't grow on trees, I had heard somewhere once, and decided to agree that meant we didn't need them.

With only our own experiences in mind, my husband and I discussed the options on the adoption paperwork and made our selections; I figured I could do some research while we waited for a match and got to know the birth mother considering us as adoptive parents.

Although I didn't know it at the time, the day I found the red-backed salamander eggs, my son was already well into his third trimester. His tail bud had come and gone, along with the webbing of his fingers and toes. His crown-rump length was eighteen inches. In fact, on the day I'd exchanged glances with a larva of *Plethodon cinereus*—though I was as yet unaware—my son's pupils had developed enough that, should they be exposed to light, they would effectively dilate.

I vowed to check the red-backed salamander eggs only once a week for the duration of their six-week maturation. I didn't want to disturb their habitat, turn their home into a jigsaw puzzle as I had the log that housed the snails. I did, however, want to see the hatchlings, a set of infinitesimally small red-backed salamander octuplets.

But I couldn't keep away. I went every couple days— sometimes every day—lifting off the top half of the log like a gift box I could keep reopening, although the log never again held as much bounty as it had that first time. Then, one day, the salamander mother disappeared. A few days after that, so did her eggs. What had happened? I read that other red-backed salamanders would sometimes cannibalize the eggs, but also that brooding females would bite, snap, and lunge at conspecifics to keep them away. If intruded upon by ring-necked snakes, though, the mothers offered no defense: females deserted their eggs in these situations 80 percent of the time in experiments, both in the lab and in the field. Occasionally, but rarely, females would pick up and move their eggs when a nest was exposed. Other times, they would eat the eggs themselves. The eggs could have hatched and I had missed them, but this was unlikely without the female present. I knew what I had here was just a correlation: too many possibilities existed for me to be sure what had happened. But I worried I had been the independent variable, that my uncurbed desire to watch the red-backed salamander larva develop had caused them to die.

*

My research on the effects of (or correlations with) the factors I had checked on the adoption application, as often happens with research, begat more questions than answers.

We all know the number one rule of pregnancy: smoking, alcohol, and drug abuse have negative effects on a developing fetus. But it is less well-known that some studies indicate positive effects in the offspring of mothers who identify as "light drinkers," such as increased attention and cognitive function. In one study, children of mothers who consumed two to six drinks per week in the first three months of pregnancy fared better on measures of positive behavior at age fourteen than children of those who did not drink at all during the first trimester.

Second to our knowledge of the negative effects of smoking, alcohol, and drug abuse during pregnancy, when thinking about things that can "wreck" our children, is our awareness that mental illnesses—in particular, schizophrenia—tend to run in families. But I found other factors not listed on the adoption application that could have just as strong an effect on, or association with, psychopathology in offspring. For instance, factors as common as being over- or under-weight or experiencing fever or infection while pregnant, as one article says in a quite causal statement, "adversely influence normal fetal neurodevelopment." So, too, does simple stress.

Stress during pregnancy, I was surprised to find, is associated with multiple negative postnatal symptoms in the child. According to Vivette Glover's research review, "Prenatal Stress and the Origins of Psychopathology," children of mothers who experience prenatal stress are at a higher risk for attention deficit/hyperactivity disorder; conduct disorder; altered function of the HPA axis; cognitive deficits; mixed-handedness; dermatoglyphic asymmetry; schizophrenia; and autism. The HPA axis contributes to height, weight, and head circumference; in infants exposed to prenatal stress, these are generally lower. Mixed-handedness means changing hand preference depending on the task; this is associated with ADHD and problems with language, school, and mental health. Dermatoglyphic asymmetry refers to uneven fingerprints, a higher incidence of which have been found in those with psychological disturbances. Many of these studies, according to Glover, have controlled for mothers' education, smoke and alcohol exposure, baby's birth weight, prematurity, and the mothers' mood after the baby's birth—all those lurking third variables. Thus, according to Glover, the research leans toward causation.

Most alarming, a mother's stress levels need not be that high to have negative effects on her developing child. (Negative, of course, is a relative term. The theory is that the babe in the mother's womb is prepared for the world the mother is living in. If born to a stressful environment, aspects of ADHD such as heightened attention could be adaptive.) Some of this data comes from studies of children conceived during well-known and traumatic historical events, such as the Dutch Hunger Winter of 1944–1945 and China's Great Leap Forward famine of 1959–1961, others from more recent natural and unnatural disasters, such as the 1998 Canadian Ice Storm and 9/11 in the US. One might expect adverse effects on children conceived and gestating during such tragedies. But other studies looked at more common life events such as debt, having a friend or family member with drug and alcohol problems, separation from a partner, and family illness or death. According to one study, mothers who experienced just three (versus one or two) stressful events during pregnancy had children with an increased risk of psychopathology. The authors of "Stress During Pregnancy Is Associated with Developmental Outcome in Infancy" found that even mild stressors such as "pregnancy-specific anxiety and increased daily hassles" can have adverse effects on the developing child. They defined pregnancy-specific anxiety as fear of the pain of giving birth or fear that the child would not be healthy. To measure the effect of daily hassles, they used a tool called the Everyday Problem List, which includes items such as "You could not find important belongings" and "You were trapped in a traffic jam." Just the stress that comes with being pregnant—the stress that comes with being *alive*—is bad for the baby. And to further complicate things, other studies have indicated that mild to moderate stress actually correlates with increased attention, motor development, and cognitive function in the child. In other words, being too relaxed during pregnancy is just as bad as being too anxious.

With this in mind, I thought about the boxes my husband and I checked, or didn't check, on the adoption paperwork. At this point, the list of characteristics to consider seemed to be more an indication of our fears and expectations, our thinking biases, or worst-case scenarios, than an accurate and practical summary of any researched-based knowledge. Nowhere do the papers ask you to indicate whether you are willing to parent a child born to a mother who experienced the death of a close relative while pregnant, a high fever, an infection, an ice storm, who is under- or overweight, vitamin D deficient, too laid-back, a nondrinker (versus a light drinker), who was often stuck in traffic, or who lost a cherished memento sometime in the first three months of her pregnancy—all of which could beget less than what you might hope for your child.

Because of my apparent carelessness with the red-backed salamander eggs I had discovered, I needed to know that somewhere, red-backed salamanders were being properly incubated and born. I returned to the forested hill above the pond and, remembering my lesson of looking within things rather than beneath, began to search. Mosquitoes and biting gnats buzzed around me, too close in the humid air. My long sleeves and long pants—my pants tucked into my socks to keep out the ticks, topped with heavy leather high-top boots to make it difficult for the ticks to grasp on—and even my hat string, clasped tightly under my neck so the hat brim bent to protect my ears, made me so hot I just didn't feel like bending over. I ignored every rule I'd ever taught my students about preserving habitats (*take only pictures, leave only footprints*) when I had worked in environmental education and kicked open with my boot every dead log in that single wet area. After fifteen minutes of this sweaty lumbering, I looked around at the obvious destruction.

A black bear could have done this, I reasoned. I'm no worse than a hungry bear.

My cell phone rang, breaking my stupor. I answered it.

"What's the plan for dinner?" my husband asked, kindly, and I felt ashamed. I had nothing to offer him. I hadn't found even one red-backed salamander.

✳

It's not just the general public and careless (or sensationalist) journalists who commit the correlation/causation fallacy. A 2006 article published in the *American Educational Research Journal* found a decrease in studies of experimental design (i.e. studies that *can* reveal causation) over a twenty-year span, yet an increase in causal statements used by researchers. The scientists themselves, they noted—even though some acknowledged that no causal inferences could be drawn—used causal language when discussing their results. Similarly, a 2004 article from the *Journal of Counseling Psychology*, which reviewed nonexperimental studies published in the journal in 2001, found that in most, researchers explained their results in causal language. In terms of their diction, scientists are, it seems, like the rest of us: cognitive misers. We know when a study does not prove causation; we understand the correlation/causation fallacy. But we also know we are going to go there anyway, to take that mental leap, because as humans we are always on the lookout for urgrund—the root cause of things. That's where the hypothesis that sparks the study—correlational or experimental—comes from in the first place: because someone thinks they know the cause of something. Our thinking biases drive not just our results but also our hypotheses. In the case of adoption, as stated by Harold D. Grotevant and Jennifer M. McDermott in the *Annual Review of Psychology*, there exists "a striking paucity of research on positive outcomes or strengths of adopted children; this stands in sharp contrast to the large literature on problem behavior and psychopathology." We tend to look only for what we already think is happening.

We should be rightfully intrigued by correlations but mindful of the correlation/causation fallacy. We should pay heed to the causes and effects science uncovers for us through sound experimental research, but we should also remember that human behavior is so complex, it's difficult to prove—because there likely isn't—a single cause for much of anything. Basing our every decision on the results of scientific research isn't a sure bet to beget us the lives we want to lead. And if you want to throw all your cause-effect thinking out the window, all the possibility of controlling the factors that you can for a healthy, happy life, consider the argument of Nobel laureate Gerard 't Hooft: there exists a deeper, deterministic set of physical laws beneath quantum mechanics that defeats its apparent uncertainty and means we have no free will anyway.

My son arrived on Sunday, August 17, 2014, while I sat in the woods with a snail on my leg. No salamanders lurked in the dry end-of-summer heat, so I had plucked up this snail from the leaf-shaded forest floor and set him upon my knee for a little observation. A few hours away, my son's birth mother rushed to the hospital with severe, unexplained pain. Called by the medical community "surprise pregnancies," "cryptic pregnancies," and—more judgmentally—"denied pregnancies," unawareness of pregnancy until labor begins is uncommon, but not rare. A 1995 German study documented one such birth in every 2,455 women, a rate three times the occurrence of triplets.

We found out about our son's birth on Monday, August 18, 2014, when the adoption agency called to tell us we had twenty-four hours, if we decided to accept the placement, to come and get him. That night, we drove to the city through torrential rain, interspersed with rainbows. We met briefly, pleasantly, with his birth parents. Then, in the nursery, a nurse handed the baby over to us with a cart of supplies, saying, "You gotta watch this one; he likes to spit up about an hour after he eats."

All I had—at least initially—to lead my research on what begets what were a few hurried notes summarizing what the birth mother had shared with the nurses, which my husband had scribbled on a tiny piece of scrap paper when he received the call from the agency. All my research was entirely after-the-fact. But it didn't matter: this little boy is marvelous.

Six months later, in our living room on a visit, his birth mother asks, "Developmentally, is he okay?"

"We think he's a genius!" my husband responds.

"I was concerned because of the lack of prenatal care," she explains.

I begin: "Humans have been having babies unassisted—"

"—for a long time," his birth father finishes.

We are all on board. This little boy seemed—for all four of us: birth and adoptive parents—to spontaneously generate. Unbeknownst to anyone, even his birth mother, for thirty-seven weeks, he had forged his way, progressing from a free-floating ball of about one hundred dividing cells to a seven-pound, fourteen-ounce infant with a dimpled X on the plump palm of each foot, which my husband and I liken to the X on the back of a spring peeper. No one knew he was coming and then all of a sudden he was there, sprung forth fully formed as if from Zeus's thigh. *Post hoc, ergo propter hoc.* In this instance I wholly submit to a failure of logic, because it gives him a beautiful lineage: *and snail begat salamander, and salamander begat storm, and storm begat rainbow, out of which came he.* And isn't the same true for life itself? After all is said and done, we *did* spring from the nonliving. Not from moldy grain, rotten meat, or the flooded Nile but from methane, ammonia, hydrogen, water, and lightning, which begat amino acids, the building blocks of protein, which begat something organized and self-replicating, which begat you and me.

SEEKING
RESEMBLANCE

When I take out the dog to do her business, my one-year-old son points to our barn, which houses an antique tractor, and repeats in a soprano voice, rolling the *r*—as if this is the only way he can squeak it out—"Carrr! Carrr! Carrr!" It is his first word, a general term he uses for anything with wheels (a hose reel, the high chair) and anything that sounds like a car (an airplane, strong wind). I'd hoped for something more natural—"tree" or "sun" or "flower"—or, of course, "momma," having waited years for the role, my husband and I finally choosing to adopt in our late thirties. But car it is. I carry him toward the barn.

Walking through my flat, central Wisconsin backyard always, somehow, transports me to the land I grew up in: the more hilly terrain of central Maryland. Our view of a ridge made up of glacial till, pocked with kames and kettles concealed by trees, makes me think—sometimes out loud—*That could be an Appalachian foothill.* At least it seems so, its upper half lit with the setting sun's horizontal rays. When I turn my car off the route that runs along the ridge and descend on the curvy road that leads to my house, I think: *This could be an Appalachian valley.* Sitting on the porch in my front yard, I can see a second ridge, one of a series formed from the glacier's recession—its edge melting and depositing, refreezing, then melting and depositing again. Though created entirely differently, it makes the general vicinity seem not so unlike Maryland's ridge-and-valley region. And when I pull out of my driveway and turn east, a drumlin covered in deciduous forest reminds me of Maryland's rolling hills, albeit solo. I can see now, after ten years, why I settled here—not in this state, but in this spot: it looks like where I came from. *It could almost be where I came from.* It isn't. Maryland was never glaciated, a topic I have written about to exhaustion: how the landscape of my adulthood differs from that of my childhood. Nevertheless, I see here a familiar geography.

In the barn, I sit my son on the cobwebbed seat of the tractor, an act that silences him, as if he had no idea that words, beyond naming things, could command action.

"Tractor," I say. "Has wheels, like a car." I pat the cracked tires, caressing the deep treads. At this point, though, approximations will do; he has no concern for exactness. And neither do I: through the open barn door, the foothill—or rather, drumlin—pleasantly obscures my view of the horizon.

"I know this is silly," my husband's aunt says one day, as she watches our son pull up and cruise around the coffee table in my in-laws' living room, "but he looks like you, Tom."

It isn't the first time we have heard this. Aunts, colleagues, nieces, a brother's mother-in-law have all said—and keep saying—the same thing: "This doesn't make sense, but he looks just like you."

As adoptive parents, my husband and I were totally unprepared for others' continuous insistence that our son looks just like us—or, at least, just like my husband. After ten years of infertility (3,560 days to concede there would never be a child that looked just like us) and several months of conscientious self-education about adoptive parenting (including preparation for transracial parenting; a factor in 28 percent of domestic adoptions), we seem to have developed a significantly different lens than that of our friends and relatives through which to view our family. We don't need physical resemblance to bind us together. We see ourselves as what we are: an adoptive family, nothing less and nothing more than any other family.

Perhaps our straightforwardness about being an adoptive family is due to the fact that our son's adoption is open. Close to 95 percent of domestic US adoptions today have some level of openness, a number that has steadily increased since the mid-twentieth century, when social mores shrouded the majority of adoptions in secrecy. In most states, open adoption basically involves nonbinding agreements not enforceable by law, and can mean anything from occasional letters and phone calls to visits between adoptive families and birth parents. For us it meant that a few days after we picked up our son, his birth parents friended us on Facebook. We don't use Facebook for much other than posting pictures of intriguing nature finds and keeping up with family (which they now were), so we figured it would be an easy way to share photos and message with them privately to plan visits.

According to Judith Modell, author of *Kinship with Strangers: Adoption and Interpretations of Kinship in American Culture*, open adoption undermines adoption's typical historical attempt to mimic blood relations; open adoption changes what it means to be a family, what it means to be related. Yet, despite our open adoption, it seems some of our friends and family members can't help but see us as a biological family. I suppose the resemblance they comment on is true at some level: as it turns out, my husband and son both have pale skin, blonde hair, and blue eyes. But when I look at my son, I see Facebook news feed pictures of his birth father. Likewise, the names my husband and I throw around at home regarding our son's looks are not ours but the names of his birth parents (I'll call them Sam and Moira). We did not know them until the day after our son's birth, but we have visited with them now a handful of times. "I feel like I'm carrying around a mini Sam!" I'll sometimes say, or "With that hat on and expression, he looks just like Moira!" And Tom, smiling and shaking his head in no less wonder than his aunt that day in his parents' living room, will respond, "I know!"

The belief that human infants closely resemble their fathers—even more so than their mothers—is common. Cross-culturally, family members of newborns, from both sides, are known to make this claim. A 1995 study in the journal *Nature* found that subjects could more easily match photos of twelve-month-old babies with photos of their fathers than with photos of their mothers. Evolutionary psychology would predict as much. While a mother can be certain an infant is hers, a father can't. Therefore, an infant who signals paternity by looking like his father might reap greater parenting benefits from his father and his father's family.

But later research—studies in 1999, 2000, and 2007 in *Evolution and Behavior*, by multiple authors—failed to replicate these results. As Paola Bressan points out in "Why Babies Look Like Their Daddies: Paternity Uncertainty and the Evolution of Self-deception in Evaluating Family Resemblance," the equation might not be so simple. Sometimes a baby's father is not a woman's monogamous mate. Thus, it may be more adaptive for a baby, at least at first, to look anonymous. Women, because they need their mates' investment in parenting, *claim* their babies look like their mates—and men, who do not wish to be cuckolded, believe them. Family members from both sides of the union, sharing the same wishes (all subconsciously, of course) reiterate the claims. Perhaps this explains the words my husband and I so often hear regarding our son's looks—and our own words when we comment that he looks like Sam: they are simply an evolved response to the illusionist that is every baby.

Even though my husband, a Wisconsin native, is weary of my comparisons of the upper Midwest's geography to that of the mid-Atlantic, in which the Midwest—in my eyes—nearly always falls short, I must repeat here a statistic that I have written about ad nauseam since moving here: Wisconsin has thirteen thousand natural lakes; Maryland has none. It would seem that in this respect, Wisconsin has the upper hand with regard to natural beauty, but I am a lover of *moving* water. Streams cannot be as easily counted as lakes because of how they join continuously into larger and larger rivers—a sort of reverse genealogy—on their journeys to the sea, which is both destination and place of origin. So I have no neat quantitative comparison for streams in Wisconsin versus streams in Maryland. But I can tell you that where I grew up, every valley had a stream; not so, here. In the glaciated portion of Wisconsin, there aren't many valleys to move streams along.

Notwithstanding what I know about this landscape, for my first five years after moving to Wisconsin, I searched for streams in the small ripples of the state's terra firma. Even today, the place I hike to most often with my son is a brook. Really, it's the tiny outlet of one lake, and inlet of another—a tenth of a mile or so of running water. But it babbles to me like a long-lost relative.

"Car, car, car," my son says, pointing to each tree as we walk there, even though I know he can make the "t" sound, and also that he knows full well these are not cars, nor have anything in common with them. He has learned that "car" is an opening for conversation, that it elicits a response, always, from my husband and me. It's an easy way for him to ask a question.

"Birch," I say and lean close to one so he can touch the smooth, white bark from his seat in the infant carrier strapped to my waist and shoulders. "Lenticels," I say, pointing to the dark, rougher, horizontal strips that cut across it.

We arrive at the brook, and my dog, Betsy, wades in for a drink. I lift my son out of the carrier, remove his shoes, roll up his pants, and plop him down on a rock in the center, his feet in the cool water. He splashes happily, teetering a bit, and begins a small rock collection, picking up stones from the bottom and examining them before—thankfully—putting them on the rock next to him rather than in his mouth. Betsy moves in and out of the water.

I watch the two of them. It seems silly, but a popular stereotype holds that people look like their dogs, and research has actually supported this. In a study oddly similar to the one in which subjects matched pictures of infants to their fathers, psychologist Sadahiko Nakajima of Kwansei Gakuin University in Japan showed that people were able to correctly pair pictures of dogs with their owners 80 percent of the time. How could such a resemblance come to be? Probably only because like picks like. I'm not sure Betsy looks like me, but family and friends have jokingly said we're alike in nature: wallflowers in the house and both of us always longing to be on a trail somewhere.

✳

Sometimes, when I can't sleep at night, I pick a trail I've known at some point in my life and hike it in my mind, putting one foot down and then the next, passing every root and rock I remember until sleep comes. Now, I often mentally travel the path to my son: failing to get pregnant; considering adoption; resigning to just wait and see, and live life as a family of two; traveling and getting degrees and saving money and sleeping in and reading and nurturing our hobbies; suddenly realizing we still wanted to be parents; reconsidering adoption; and then, just three weeks post-home study, receiving a call for an emergency placement. A baby had been born; we had been chosen by his birth parents; we needed to buy a car seat and come to the hospital to pick up our son.

Our son. When did we first begin to conceive of him this way? To regard ourselves as parents? Anthropologist Signe Howell coined the term "kinning" to describe the process by which any new person—adult or child, adopted or biological—"is brought into a significant and permanent relationship with a group of people that is expressed in a kin idiom." She proclaims kinning a "universal process," meaning all societies engage in it—like language or funeral rites.

Kinning, Howell posits, involves both nature and nurture. In one indigenous Ecuadorean community studied by Mary Weismantel in "Making Kin: Kinship Theory and Zumbagua Adoptions," for example, "a child can be physically made one's own by eating the same food over time, by sharing emotional states, and by being in close physical proximity to people and objects." This contrasts sharply with beliefs about kinship in Western cultures, which tend to define kinship by biology—shared characteristics passed along through DNA. So how do adoptive families residing in genetic essentialist cultures manage to kin their biologically unconnected children?

Surprisingly enough, they do it, Howell observes, with relative ease, sometimes holding their children's characteristics in the foreground and sometimes in the background, depending on the context. Howell's extensive research about the process of kinning mostly focuses on transnational adoption, in which the physical appearance of the child often presents a strong visual message regarding biological relatedness within the adoptive family. But as the mother of a domestically adopted child who can see my son's birth parents' features—but not my own—in my son's face, I think Howell's observations about kinning apply here too. While it is always assumed adopted children look most like their biological parents, Howell observes that adopted children and their parents begin a "quest for resemblances"—for example, in physique or personality. And though it is understood that the adopted child could have been placed with other adoptive parents and vice versa, most adoptive families create backstories that imply fate was a factor in their placements. Howell likens the process of kinning to transubstantiation—the changing of one substance into another. It is, quite fittingly, a kind of communion, an important ritual. When someone is kinned, though their appearance stays the same, a fundamental change takes place.

"Good for you!" a woman commented, when I passed her last winter about two miles in on Wisconsin's Ice Age Trail, snowshoes buckled to my feet, baby strapped to my belly. He was heavy—eighteen pounds at four months—and I sometimes thought about the weight as we walked, tried to imagine he was under my skin and not just under my coat, mused about how long it would take me to equal, in hikes like these, nine months of carrying him. But pregnancy was—and always will be—beyond me. I can't imagine it. And the truth is, it doesn't matter.

What matters is that I was in the woods with my son. And gradually, on these walks, he began to sleep less and observe more. I sat him down on frozen ponds for photoshoots next to snow-covered mounds wherein warm muskrats slept. We unearthed blue-spotted salamanders from beneath decomposing logs and looked at each other in matched amazement, me saying, "Yes, isn't this an unbelievable planet we live on?"

It has been not the internal but the external world that has made me a parent. It has been these shared walks through the woods, these moments of discovery, of wonder, that have made us mother and son.

Adoption is a legal fiction. This is, according to the law, how it is categorized. Just like corporate "personhood," it is an assertion accepted as true in order to achieve a particular goal in a legal matter. Corporations, though they are not persons, can have residences, nationalities, and even enemies. Through adoption, infertile couples can have children.

In Wisconsin, after the thirty-day period in which birth parents may reconsider their choice of adoption, adoptive parents wait six months until, in a court hearing, the child legally becomes theirs. Usually, a new birth certificate is issued along with the adoption decree. During our hearing, although I had schooled myself in the legal proceedings, I was surprised at the judge's words: "Do you understand that we will be amending the birth certificate as if he was born to you?"

I nodded, but inside I felt shocked: this wasn't what I wanted at all. Yes, I wanted our son to have our last name; I wanted the legal document that says we are his parents, that protects our ability to be a family; I wanted the whole process to be over. But I did not want to erase my son's origin story. In my mind, his birth certificate should be more like a marriage certificate, with the names of his birth parents *and* his adoptive parents. *Born to* and *son of* I had imagined it might say, though I must have known this wouldn't be the case.

Over the course of the next year, I watched my son's birth parents through the curious window that Facebook provides. They posted picture after picture that I could have posted myself: camping, sunsets, shorelines, links to news articles on social and political issues that I completely agreed with. I know Facebook does not reveal a completely accurate picture of anyone's life, but in this case, it seems, like did pick like.

One night, they texted us photos of the two of them when they were little. My husband and I could see the resemblances already and hoped they would continue—a promise of lop-sided, golden curls falling from his head. We showed the pictures to my husband's mother, but she only frowned a little, and said nothing. My best friend refused to look at them. I decided not to even mention them to my own family.

One day, our son's birth father invited us to meet his parents at their family's lake house. Moira made brunch, and as we sat around the table, Sam's mother mentioned how my husband and her son kind of look like each other. To lay this out more clearly, this was our son's birth grandmother pointing out that her grandchild's adoptive father resembles her son. For a moment, we all stared at the two of them.

There was no mention of any resemblance between Moira and me. Maybe we truly don't look alike. Maybe we don't expect little boys to resemble adult females. Or was it because there is absolute proof which one of us mothered this little boy for the first nine months of his life? No need, and therefore no evolved mechanism, for discussing how much a baby looks like its mother?

We spent the rest of the morning outside, letting our son explore the yard and shoreline of the lake. Someone pointed to a patch of long-stemmed, fiery-orange dandelion-like flowers in a soggy corner of the lawn. Moira called them something not found in this region, a popular western species that looks similar—in fact, I had misidentified them the same way at one point. I knew what they really were but held back. It wasn't my place, I felt, to be saying what was what. And what does it matter what you call something, its true species, genus, and family? The greater truth is that the flower is gorgeous; we all loved it. Instead, I told them how it also grows on our lawn, and I, too, mow around it.

Sam and his dad pulled a little ride-on car out of the shed, which one of my son's birth cousins had outgrown. They told us to keep it, and we thanked them. Later, as we unpacked the car, we found a cone of red pine that Sam had also placed in our trunk. I set it in front of the picture of Sam and Moira that we placed in our son's room.

Research in the '80s and '90s, when closed adoption was the norm, revealed that almost all surveyed domestic adoptees and birth parents desired reunions with each other—hence the development of open adoption. Interestingly, however, research shows that a low percentage of people adopted transnationally desire reunions with their birth parents.

Instead, they seem to desire reunions with their "birth countries," as if the land itself were the architect of identity, as if the earth had labored to produce them. Of course, the traditional high-school graduation present of a trip to the birth country for transnational adoptees is more about culture than geography. But landscapes have a way of making us who we are too.

After a decade of living in Wisconsin, I have begun to acclimate to its thirteen thousand lakes, or, at least, to one of them: Sunset Lake, a deep, clear glacial lake with a public beach a few miles from our house. All summer long, I take my son there and put him in one of those inner-tubes for babies and set him in the water where, at the right depth, he can walk. His first hike is in a lake.

On Labor Day, it becomes unexpectedly and seriously hot enough to propel me to the lake, despite the fact that it's a holiday and I know it will be crowded. It's a late-afternoon, spur-of-the-moment decision, and I don't even put a shirt on over my halter-style swim top. On my feet is a pair of plastic, bejeweled flip-flops I've put on just for short jaunts from car to beach and back again. I've put my son in a swim shirt and swim trunks, and rather than squeeze him into a thick, uncomfortable swim diaper, for the first time I've left him dangerously diaperless. But when we arrive at the lake, what I've feared is true: it's too crowded. There is no place to park and no space to swim either.

We're not dressed for hiking, but I'm itching to be outdoors. I make a quick decision and drive past the lake to the Ice Age trailhead. This is the first time I've hiked with my son without aid of a carrier, and, swim tops slipping, we sweat against one another, skin-on-skin as I grunt up the hills in the heat. I gingerly navigate my steps, my toes threatening to slip off the edge of my flip-flops.

At the bottom of a hill, where a short boardwalk crosses a simmering wetland, I pause to catch my breath, slide my son down my sweaty leg, and place him between my feet. Several frogs jump, squeaking, into the water. Agrimony, a tall yellow wildflower, blooms nearby. I point these things out, gems of the forest, but he is totally absorbed by some other object. My flip-flop.

"We didn't come here to examine the fake plastic jewel on my flip-flops," I tell him, then smile. Maybe we did. It's like our first trip to the zoo, where I was hard-pressed to get him, at nine months, to notice a giraffe, elephant, or ostrich, but he was fascinated by the fences and the young humans. This is the beauty of his age, a little bit of which I wish he—we all—could keep: our alien-on-a-new-planet perspective, our un-enculturation. He knows nothing of relevance—or of relatives, for that matter. At his age anything is possible, anything could be normal, even having two parents biologically unrelated to him.

＊

My son's second word is "daddy." He says it one evening when we are stepping out of the car, all three of us, from some errand. After months of multisyllabic dada's, he looks at my husband and smiles and says "Daddeee" not as if it is the first time, but as if they are being reunited after a long absence. "Daddeee, Daddeee," we get for weeks. Occasionally, he will call me "Daddeee" too.

The seasons change and the ground freezes. My son weighs thirty pounds and I can no longer carry him far on my front, so my husband helps me position him in the carrier on my back, and then the two of us—just my son and I—walk through the yard past the barn and over the frozen furrows of the cornfield, through a narrow pine plantation, and up to the top of the steep, round kame that from our house still reminds me of an Appalachian foothill.

The physical comparisons no longer surprise or bother me. If making mountains out of moraines and making brooks out of lake inlets has helped me to adjust to the Midwestern landscape, how can I mind when other people liken my husband to my son in order to view us as his parents? Transubstantiation is hard. When I look at my son, what is appearance and what is reality flips back and forth in my mind until I can't figure out where the sleight of hand is. I don't know how else to say this other than that my son is both my son and someone else's. For me, it amounts to a sort of reverse communion, a new riff on an old adage: blood is thicker than water, yes, but blood is also *mostly* water. Over 80 percent. This is the bigger picture. The relatedness of the people in the photo depends on the frame of reference.

Anthropologist Sidsel Roalkvam has said that kinship "creates continuity over time, and gives people a sense of 'belonging to a life,' to something bigger than the individual." That is how I feel when I look at my son—as if I am looking to the edge of the universe, back in time, at some curve of cheek or nose-bridge or raised eyebrow that has survived through all the myriad individuals sexual reproduction allows. Resemblance is proof of so many things we cannot see: that double helix, the mixing of two people that sparks our existence. In my son's resemblance to his birth parents lies something I admire: a certain staying power—not my own or anybody's in particular—just the beauty of what gets passed down and sticks around. That this happens at all gives me solace.

To get home from our hike, I lift my son from my back and carefully carry him halfway down the steepest part of the kame, then sit him on his butt, and he slides the rest of the way on his own, laughing and pointing at the dog and saying her nickname, "Bubbles"—his third word—over and over. Then, for the last little part of our journey, I strap him over my belly and carry him home.

The *Journal* Non/Fiction Prize
(formerly The Ohio State University Prize in Short Fiction)